The Complete Guide to
UX Design
for Beginners

A Step-by-Step Introduction to User Experience Design Thinking Principles and Practices

CHAD SCOTT

All rights reserved. No part of this publication may be reproduced, redistributed, or transmitted in any form or by any means, including photocopying, recording, or other electronic or mechanical methods, without the prior written permission of the publisher, except in the case of brief quotations embodied in critical reviews and certain other noncommercial uses permitted by copyright law.

Copyright © 2024 CHAD SCOTT

Table of Content

Table of Content..2
Introduction..5
Part 1...12
Understanding the Foundations of UX Design...
12
Chapter 1..13
What is UX Design? Key Concepts...................13
Chapter 2... 21
The Key Differences Between UX and UI Design
.... 21
Chapter 3..30
Building the Right Mindset for a UX Career...30
Part 2...39
The Design Thinking Process for UX Beginners.
39
Chapter 4..40
Introduction to Design Thinking......................40
Chapter 5..49
User Research Fundamentals..........................49
Chapter 6..58
Step 1 - Empathize with the User..................... 58
Chapter 7..66
Step 2 - Define the Problem............................66
Chapter 8..74

Step 3 - Ideate and Brainstorm Solutions....... 74
Chapter 9...82
Step 4 - Prototype Your Design....................... 83
Chapter 10.. 93
Step 5 - Test and Refine the Prototype............ 93
Part 3... 100
Essential UX Design Principles and Best Practices... 100
Chapter 11... 101
Core UX Design Principles Every Beginner Should Know (Usability, Accessibility, Visual Hierarchy)..101
Chapter 12.. 108
Accessibility in UX: Designing for Everyone. 108
Chapter 13... 116
Case Studies: Lessons from Real UX Projects 116
Part 4.. 124
Developing Practical Skills and Building Your Portfolio.. 124
Chapter 14.. 125
Effective Communication in UX Design: Visual and Verbal Skills...125
Chapter 15.. 132
Building a Compelling UX/UI Portfolio: Showcase Your Work...132
Chapter 16... 141

3

Essential Tools and Resources for UX Designers (Research, Wireframing, Prototyping Tools). 141

Part 5 150

Preparing for a Successful UX Career............150

Chapter 17.. 151

Creating a Clear UX Career Roadmap: Setting Goals and Objectives..151

Chapter 18... 160

Networking and Freelancing in UX: Insights and Strategies..160

Chapter 19...169

The Future of UX Design: Trends and Technologies to Watch................................... 169

Appendices..179

Introduction

The digital world is evolving at a breakneck pace, and with it, the field of User Experience (UX) design has grown into one of the most impactful and sought-after disciplines. Whether you're here because you're curious about UX, considering a career shift, or simply want to understand what UX designers do, you're in the right place. This book is crafted to guide you through the foundational aspects of UX design, using clear, simple language and practical examples to demystify a field that, while complex, is ultimately all about understanding people and making their digital interactions easier and more enjoyable.

At its core, UX design is all about the user—their needs, their frustrations, and ultimately, their satisfaction. A good UX designer makes navigating a website, using an app, or interacting with any digital product as intuitive and enjoyable as possible. It's a blend of psychology, design, and technology, and mastering it can open doors to a rewarding and innovative career.

In this book, we'll explore the five-step design thinking process used by successful UX designers worldwide and break down the skills, tools, and mindset needed to start your journey in UX design. Whether you're looking to enhance your understanding of digital experiences or are ready to dive into a new field, this guide will provide the foundation you need to get started.

Why UX Design Matters for Businesses and Designers

Why do some apps and websites draw people in, while others push them away? Why do some businesses thrive online while others struggle to hold their audience? Much of the answer lies in UX design. A well-designed user experience is no longer a luxury—it's a necessity. Here's why UX design matters and how it impacts businesses and designers alike:

For Businesses: User Experience Is Key to Success

1. **Customer Satisfaction and Loyalty**

   A well-crafted user experience keeps people coming back. When a customer finds a website or app easy to navigate and enjoyable to use, they're more likely to return and engage with the brand. Studies have shown that 89% of consumers will switch to a competitor after a poor user experience. UX design directly influences user satisfaction, turning one-time visitors into loyal customers.

2. **Increased Conversion Rates**
UX design doesn't just make things look good; it can directly boost a business's bottom line. For example, research shows that well-designed UX can increase conversion rates by up to 400%. A simple, intuitive design makes it easy for users to find what they're looking for, complete purchases, or take other actions that benefit the business.

3. **Reduced Costs**
Investing in UX design early in the product development process saves companies time and money in the long run. Identifying and solving usability issues during the design phase reduces the likelihood of expensive post-launch fixes. The result? Lower development costs, fewer customer complaints, and more efficient updates and improvements.

For Designers: Building a Career with Purpose and Growth

1. **High Demand and Career Opportunities**
As more companies recognize the value of user-centered design, the demand for skilled UX designers continues to rise. A career in UX offers a wealth of opportunities across

industries—whether in tech, retail, finance, or healthcare. UX designers often find themselves in roles where they can make a real impact on the product, brand, and company's success.

2. **A Focus on Problem Solving**

   UX design is for people who love solving problems creatively. It's not just about making something look good; it's about understanding people and crafting solutions that make their lives easier. Each project presents unique challenges, making UX an exciting and fulfilling field for those who thrive on innovation and adaptability.

3. **Personal and Professional Growth**

   UX design blends technical and soft skills—understanding user psychology, collaborating with cross-functional teams, and using design tools and technologies. The field is constantly evolving, and designers must be lifelong learners, staying current with new tools, trends, and best practices. This continuous learning makes UX a rewarding and dynamic career.

Building a Beginner-Friendly UX Mindset

Diving into UX design can feel overwhelming. As a beginner, it's essential to cultivate the right mindset to navigate the challenges ahead and set yourself up for success. Here are three key aspects of a beginner-friendly UX mindset:

1. Embrace Curiosity and Empathy

Great UX designers are endlessly curious. They want to understand why people behave the way they do, what motivates them, and what frustrates them. Curiosity fuels empathy—the ability to see things from the user's perspective. By being genuinely interested in what users experience, you're more likely to create solutions that meet their needs.

To cultivate empathy, spend time learning about your audience, observing their behaviors, and understanding their pain points. Approach each project with an open mind, willing to explore different perspectives. This mindset will help you design with purpose and create experiences that resonate with users.

2. Be Open to Feedback and Continuous Learning

UX design is iterative—meaning you'll constantly test, refine, and improve your work based on user feedback. Being open to constructive criticism is vital for growth as a designer. Don't be discouraged if your initial ideas aren't perfect; instead, see every project as a learning opportunity.

The field of UX is continually evolving, with new tools, techniques, and insights emerging all the time. Staying curious and keeping up with industry trends will help you stay relevant and develop a strong design portfolio. Remember, even the most experienced designers started as beginners.

3. Focus on Solving Problems, Not Just Creating Pretty Designs
While visual design is a part of UX, the focus is always on functionality and usability. A beautiful design that doesn't serve the user's needs is ultimately ineffective. To succeed in UX, concentrate on solving real problems. Ask yourself, *"How can I make this process easier for the user?"* or *"What design choice will reduce frustration and improve satisfaction?"*

By grounding your work in purpose and function, you'll approach design with a more critical eye, making choices that benefit users and lead to better experiences. Over time, this problem-solving mindset will set you apart as a thoughtful, user-centered designer.

With the right mindset, UX design becomes more than a skill set—it's a rewarding way to impact how people interact with the digital world. As we move forward, we'll dive into each aspect of UX design, from the fundamentals to the tools and techniques that will shape your journey. Let's get started!

Part 1

Understanding the Foundations of UX Design

Chapter 1

What is UX Design? Key Concepts

In a world where digital experiences play a huge role in our daily lives, User Experience (UX) design has emerged as a critical discipline. It's not just about making things look good; it's about understanding how people interact with technology, anticipating their needs, and creating solutions that make their experience seamless and enjoyable. But what exactly is UX design? And what sets it apart from other design disciplines? Let's break down the key concepts that define UX design and help us understand its unique purpose and role in today's digital landscape.

Understanding UX Design

More Than Just Pretty Interfaces

At its core, UX design is the practice of creating digital products that are easy to use, efficient, and enjoyable. It focuses on the full experience a person has when they interact with a product, such as a website, app, or software platform. This experience encompasses everything from how quickly users find what they need, to how smoothly they can complete a task, to how satisfying and intuitive the overall interaction feels.

Unlike UI (User Interface) design, which focuses on the look and feel of a product, UX design is about understanding and shaping the entire journey a user takes. While UI is certainly a component of UX, UX encompasses the entire scope of interaction—emotions, ease of use, clarity, and even accessibility.

The Goal of UX Design

Putting the User First

The main goal of UX design is to ensure that users find value in the product they are interacting with. This means understanding users' needs, desires, motivations, and pain points. To achieve this, UX designers prioritize user-centered design, meaning every decision is made with the user in mind. This approach reduces friction, minimizes frustration, and aims to solve real problems users face.

Good UX design can have a significant impact on a business's success. A positive user experience keeps users engaged, encourages them to return, and can even convert casual visitors into loyal customers. On the other hand, a poor UX can frustrate users, resulting in them abandoning the product altogether. This is why UX design is essential for any business that wants to build strong relationships with its users.

Key Concepts in UX Design

To grasp UX design in its entirety, let's explore some of the core concepts that every UX designer needs to understand:

1. **User-Centered Design (UCD)**
   User-centered design is a design philosophy that puts the user at the forefront of every decision. It means that instead of focusing solely on what looks good or fits business goals, UX designers take the time to understand who the users are, what they need, and how the product can serve them effectively. This approach leads to products that feel natural to use and are genuinely helpful to the user.
2. **Usability**
   Usability is a cornerstone of UX design. It refers to how easy it is for users to interact with a product and achieve their goals. If a product has high usability, users can complete tasks quickly and with minimal effort. Poor usability, on the other hand, can lead to frustration, errors, and abandonment. Usability testing is a common

practice in UX design to measure and improve this aspect of the user experience.

3. **Accessibility**

   Accessibility ensures that products are usable by people of all abilities, including those with disabilities. UX designers aim to create products that are inclusive and can be used by a diverse audience. This means considering visual, auditory, physical, and cognitive accessibility when designing. Accessibility is not just a moral obligation; in many regions, it's also a legal requirement for digital products.

4. **Information Architecture (IA)**

   Information architecture is the organization and structuring of content in a way that helps users find information and complete tasks with ease. In UX design, IA involves deciding how information is grouped, labeled, and presented on a product. The goal is to create a structure that makes sense to users and guides them through their journey without confusion.

5. **Interaction Design (IxD)**

   Interaction design focuses on how users interact with a product and how the product responds to those interactions. It's about designing interactive elements, like buttons, navigation menus, forms, and gestures, in a way that feels intuitive. A well-designed interaction flow allows users to perform actions smoothly, providing clear feedback and keeping users engaged.

6. **Visual Design**

    Although it's often thought of as separate from UX, visual design is an important aspect of the user experience. Visual design is about creating a product that is not only functional but also visually appealing. It includes elements like color schemes, typography, layout, and imagery. Good visual design enhances the overall experience by making the product feel cohesive, polished, and pleasant to use.

7. **User Research**

    User research is the foundation of UX design. It involves gathering insights about users, their behavior, needs, and motivations. UX designers use techniques like surveys, interviews, usability testing, and observation to understand users deeply. This information guides design decisions, ensuring they are based on real user needs rather than assumptions.

8. **Prototyping and Testing**

    Prototyping is the process of creating a preliminary version of a product to test and validate ideas. It allows designers to experiment with different solutions, gather user feedback, and make improvements before launching the final product. Testing these prototypes with actual users helps identify issues and refine the design, ultimately leading to a better user experience.

The UX Process

An Iterative Journey

UX design is rarely a linear process; it's iterative. This means that instead of following a strict, one-way path, UX designers revisit and refine each step multiple times based on new information and feedback. This approach allows designers to continuously improve the product, adapting it to meet evolving user needs.

An essential part of this iterative process is the five-step design thinking approach:

1. **Empathize:** Understanding users' needs, goals, and pain points.
2. **Define:** Clearly identifying the problem that the design will solve.
3. **Ideate:** Generating a wide range of creative solutions.
4. **Prototype:** Creating a testable version of the product.
5. **Test:** Gathering feedback to refine and improve the design.

Each stage informs the next, creating a cycle of continuous improvement. This process not only helps designers stay user-centered but also leads to more innovative and effective solutions.

Why UX and UI Are Often Confused

Many people use "UX" and "UI" interchangeably, but they're not the same. While UI (User Interface) design is about creating the look and feel of a product, UX design encompasses the entire user journey. Think of it this way: UX is the map guiding the user's path, while UI is the aesthetic appeal that makes that path visually enjoyable.

UI focuses on visual elements like color schemes, button styles, and font choices, while UX considers broader questions like "How can we make it easy for users to find what they're looking for?" and "What would make users feel happy and confident using this product?"

In practice, UI is a component of UX, but UX involves far more than just appearance—it's about the total experience from start to finish.

Bringing It All Together

UX design is a rich, multifaceted field that balances creativity and empathy with strategy and analysis. At its best, UX design combines art and science to create digital experiences that not only look good but serve a real purpose. It's about crafting experiences that resonate with users, solve their problems, and make their lives just a little bit easier.

With this foundation, you're well on your way to understanding the big picture of UX design. As you dive deeper into each concept, you'll see how all these elements work together to create engaging, functional, and user-centered products. Let's continue exploring the essential tools, principles, and practices that will set you up for success in the exciting world of UX design.

Chapter 2

The Key Differences Between UX and UI Design

In the design world, two terms frequently appear together: UX and UI. While they are related and often intertwined, they serve distinct purposes within the realm of digital product design. Understanding the differences between UX (User Experience) and UI (User Interface) is essential for any aspiring designer or anyone working alongside design teams. Both fields aim to create a product that users love, but they approach this goal in very different ways. Let's explore the roles of UX and UI design and clarify what each entails.

Defining UX Design: The Full Journey
User Experience (UX) design focuses on the entire journey a user takes when interacting with a product. Think of it as the roadmap that guides users from one point to another, ensuring that every interaction feels smooth, intuitive, and satisfying. UX design is about problem-solving; it involves understanding users' needs, behaviors, and

pain points to create solutions that address these factors effectively.

A UX designer's job is to make sure that every step in the user journey feels cohesive and logical. This process includes research, user testing, and iterative adjustments to make sure the design aligns with real user needs. UX design is holistic and involves a wide range of practices such as user research, information architecture, wireframing, prototyping, and usability testing. Ultimately, it's about making a product useful, accessible, and enjoyable to interact with.

Key Elements of UX Design

- **User Research:** Gathering information about user needs, motivations, and pain points.
- **Information Architecture (IA):** Structuring content and navigation so users can easily find what they need.
- **Prototyping and Wireframing:** Creating preliminary versions of a product to visualize and test ideas.
- **Usability Testing:** Gathering feedback from users to refine the design based on real-world interactions.

- **Interaction Design:** Designing how users interact with different elements, such as buttons and forms.

While UX design doesn't involve creating the visual look of a product, it deeply influences how the product functions and how users experience it. UX is focused on the *why* and *how*—why a product is used and how it meets user needs.

Defining UI Design: The Visual Aesthetic

User Interface (UI) design, on the other hand, focuses specifically on the visual aspects of a product. UI design is about crafting an interface that is visually appealing, coherent, and consistent with the brand's identity. UI designers are responsible for the look and feel of a product—the color schemes, typography, icons, images, and overall layout. Their goal is to create an interface that not only looks good but also guides the user intuitively through the product.

UI design requires an understanding of design principles like color theory, typography, and layout design. UI designers also need to consider accessibility, ensuring that the visual elements can be understood and used by a diverse range of users.

While UX design provides the foundation of the product's functionality, UI design brings it to life through aesthetics. UI designers think about how visual elements can make the product feel intuitive, memorable, and enjoyable to use.

Key Elements of UI Design
- **Visual Hierarchy:** Organizing content visually to guide the user's attention.
- **Color Theory:** Using color schemes that align with the brand and create the right mood.
- **Typography:** Choosing fonts that are legible and consistent with the product's tone.
- **Button Design and Icons:** Designing interactive elements that are easy to recognize and use.
- **Layout and Spacing:** Creating a clear and pleasing arrangement of elements on each screen.

UI design is about the *what*—what the user sees and interacts with on each page. UI designers work to make sure that every visual detail contributes to a seamless and enjoyable experience.

The Relationship Between UX and UI Design
The most effective products come from a close collaboration between UX and UI design. While UX sets the foundation and structure of a product, UI brings that structure to life in a way that is visually pleasing and easy to navigate. Think of UX as the blueprint of a building, and UI as the paint, furniture, and decor that make it inviting.

Here's how the two fields complement each other:

- **UX provides the structure; UI provides the appeal.** UX design maps out the user's journey, defining how users will interact with the product. UI design then takes this journey and makes it visually engaging.
- **UX solves problems; UI enhances experience.** UX design focuses on making a product functional and solving user pain points. UI design ensures that this functionality is delivered in a visually satisfying way.
- **UX and UI work together to build trust.** Users are more likely to feel satisfied when a product both works well and looks good. By aligning usability with aesthetics, UX and UI together create a consistent, enjoyable experience that builds user trust.

While UX can exist without UI in the form of low-fidelity wireframes or prototypes, UI without UX would lack purpose and structure, likely leading to a confusing and unsatisfying user experience.

Examples of UX and UI in Action
Let's look at a simple example—a food delivery app. The UX designer's role would involve mapping out the user journey: from opening the app to searching for restaurants, placing an order, and making payment. They would focus on making sure this process is intuitive, removing any barriers that might frustrate users.

The UI designer, meanwhile, would decide how each of these steps looks. They would choose the color scheme, design the buttons, and ensure that the visual design is inviting and aligned with the brand's identity. They might add icons to represent different food categories and use color to highlight the "Order Now" button, making it visually prominent and easy to find.

Together, UX and UI design create a seamless experience: the user can easily find and order food (thanks to UX), and they feel good doing it (thanks to UI).

Key Differences Between UX and UI Design

1. **Focus:**
   - **UX:** Concerned with the overall experience and functionality.
   - **UI:** Concerned with the visual and interactive aspects of the product.
2. **Process:**
   - **UX:** Involves user research, journey mapping, prototyping, and testing.
   - **UI:** Involves visual design, color and typography choices, and creating interactive elements.
3. **Goal:**
   - **UX:** To solve problems and ensure the product is easy to use.
   - **UI:** To make the product visually appealing and consistent with the brand.
4. **Tools Used:**
   - **UX Designers** might use tools like wireframing software (Sketch, Figma), journey mapping tools, and usability testing platforms.
   - **UI Designers** often use graphic design tools (Adobe XD, Photoshop), icon libraries, and color palette generators.

5. **Metrics of Success:**
   - **UX Success:** Measured by user satisfaction, task completion rates, and overall usability.
   - **UI Success:** Measured by visual appeal, user engagement, and consistency with brand identity.

Why Understanding Both Matters for a Beginner

While UX and UI have different roles, understanding both is essential for anyone looking to work in design. Having knowledge of both disciplines allows designers to make more informed decisions, whether they are working solely in UX, UI, or both. Knowing how they interrelate ensures that the design process is cohesive, effective, and user-centered from start to finish.

For beginners, starting with a focus on UX design provides a solid foundation in problem-solving and user research. Once you're comfortable with UX, exploring UI design will add to your skill set, making you a well-rounded designer who understands both the function and the form of digital products.

UX and UI design are two sides of the same coin, working together to create products that are not only functional but also enjoyable. While they each have unique roles and processes, they share the common goal of enhancing the user experience. For any beginner stepping into the design field, understanding these distinctions will help clarify your path and equip you to deliver more effective and engaging digital products.

As you continue learning, remember that while UX lays the groundwork, UI adds the polish. Together, they transform ideas into products that users want to return to, again and again. Now that we've covered the basics, we'll dive deeper into the design thinking process—a powerful framework to guide your UX journey from empathy to solution.

Chapter 3

Building the Right Mindset for a UX Career

Embarking on a UX design career is not just about mastering technical skills or understanding the user journey; it's about cultivating a mindset that embraces curiosity, empathy, resilience, and adaptability. These qualities set successful UX designers apart and enable them to thrive in a field that's constantly evolving. In this chapter, we'll explore the attitudes, values, and perspectives that form the foundation of a rewarding UX career, as well as some practical steps you can take to nurture this mindset.

1. Embracing Empathy: The Heart of UX Design

At its core, UX design is about understanding and solving users' problems. It requires an empathetic approach, meaning you need to put yourself in the users' shoes and consider their needs, pain points, and desires. Empathy in UX design is not just a skill; it's a mindset that drives every stage of the design process.

To build empathy, focus on the following:
- **Listen Actively:** Spend time listening to users during interviews or usability tests without making assumptions. Let users express their needs in their own words.
- **Challenge Personal Biases:** Recognize that your own preferences may differ from those of your users. Always design with the user in mind, not just based on your own intuition.
- **Seek Diverse Perspectives:** Interact with a variety of users to avoid a one-size-fits-all approach. Designing for inclusivity enhances the experience for everyone and deepens your understanding of different user needs.

Empathy is essential for effective UX design because it keeps the focus on real people. This user-centered mindset ensures that every decision aligns with the goal of improving the user's experience.

2. Developing a Curiosity for Problem-Solving

UX design is a field of inquiry and exploration. Designers often encounter new challenges that require creative problem-solving and innovative thinking. Cultivating curiosity will keep you engaged and drive you to ask "Why?" and "How?"

as you explore new ways to improve user experiences.

To foster a problem-solving mindset:
- **Ask Questions Constantly:** Whether it's about understanding a user's behavior or evaluating a design's effectiveness, never hesitate to dig deeper.
- **Analyze Failures and Successes:** Evaluate past projects, analyzing what went well and what could be improved. This reflection will provide insights for future designs.
- **Stay Updated:** UX is a fast-moving field with emerging trends, tools, and methods. Make learning a continuous process so you can adapt to industry changes and bring fresh perspectives to your work.

Curiosity ensures that you're always ready to find new, innovative solutions and to see challenges as opportunities for growth and discovery.

3. Adopting Resilience and Adaptability

UX design is an iterative process. There will be times when ideas fail, feedback is critical, or solutions don't meet user expectations. Resilience enables you to view these challenges as valuable lessons rather than setbacks. Similarly, adaptability allows you to pivot and refine your approach based on new insights.

Key tips for building resilience and adaptability include:

- **Welcome Feedback:** Feedback is a gift that can improve your work. Learn to separate your self-worth from critiques and embrace them as tools for growth.
- **Experiment Freely:** Not every idea will succeed, but each one will teach you something. Take calculated risks, and view failures as steps toward a better solution.
- **Stay Flexible:** Be prepared to adjust your designs or even start from scratch. Design is an evolving process, and flexibility allows you to stay open to changes that benefit the user experience.

With resilience, you'll be more prepared to handle setbacks, and with adaptability, you'll be able to evolve with each project, improving continuously.

4. Cultivating a Growth Mindset
In UX design, there is always more to learn. Cultivating a growth mindset means understanding that skills and abilities are not fixed; they can be developed through dedication and hard work.

Designers with a growth mindset are open to learning from experiences, committed to improving their skills, and eager to take on new challenges.

Here's how to nurture a growth mindset:
- **Set Learning Goals:** Define specific skills or knowledge you want to develop. This can range from mastering a new tool to deepening your understanding of user psychology.
- **Celebrate Small Wins:** Acknowledge your progress, even if it's incremental. Each skill you build, or project you complete brings you closer to your long-term goals.
- **Learn from Others:** Seek inspiration from other designers, participate in communities, and collaborate openly. Sharing insights can provide fresh perspectives and deepen your knowledge.

A growth mindset encourages a proactive approach to self-improvement, allowing you to continuously refine your skills and embrace the challenges of UX design.

5. Being Open to Collaboration
UX design is rarely a solo endeavor. Collaboration with developers, product managers, marketers, and other stakeholders is essential to creating cohesive and effective products. Building strong communication and collaboration skills will enable

you to work well in multidisciplinary teams and foster an environment of shared creativity.

To build a collaborative mindset:
- **Practice Clear Communication:** Be concise and transparent when explaining your design choices. Clear communication helps bridge gaps between different team members' perspectives.
- **Value Diverse Perspectives:** Each team member brings unique skills and insights. Learning from others will strengthen your work and lead to more well-rounded solutions.
- **Maintain a User-Centric Focus:** In discussions with others, always bring the conversation back to the user's needs. This shared focus helps align everyone's efforts toward the same goal.

Collaboration enriches the design process, allowing you to tap into a wealth of knowledge and perspectives that enhance the final product.

6. Focusing on Continuous Improvement
The UX field is ever-evolving, with new tools, trends, and best practices emerging regularly. To remain relevant and excel in your career, it's crucial to adopt a mindset of continuous improvement. Staying up-to-date with industry developments and honing your skills will enable you to deliver

high-quality designs and remain adaptable in a fast-changing environment.

To prioritize continuous improvement:
- **Engage with the Design Community:** Join forums, attend workshops, and participate in webinars. Engaging with others in the field can spark ideas and reveal emerging practices.
- **Seek Out Mentors and Role Models:** Learning from experienced UX designers can provide valuable insights into the challenges and rewards of a UX career.
- **Reflect on Your Work Regularly:** Take time after each project to evaluate what worked and what didn't. This reflection fosters growth and helps you refine your approach for future projects.

By focusing on improvement, you'll stay motivated, relevant, and inspired in your UX journey.

7. Practicing Patience and Humility
UX design is a journey that takes time, effort, and a willingness to learn from every experience. As you progress, patience and humility will help you navigate the complexities of design and avoid burnout. Being humble enough to learn from mistakes and take feedback constructively will keep you grounded and open to growth.

To cultivate patience and humility:
- **Celebrate Progress, Not Perfection:** Understand that design is iterative; improvements happen over time. Appreciate each small step forward.
- **Stay Humble in Your Approach:** UX design requires constant learning and unlearning. Approach each project with a beginner's mindset, ready to adapt and absorb new insights.
- **Practice Patience with Yourself:** Building expertise takes time. Allow yourself to grow gradually and enjoy the journey of self-improvement.

With patience and humility, you'll develop a resilient foundation that supports your career growth and keeps you focused on creating meaningful experiences for users.

Cultivating the right mindset for a UX career is about embracing empathy, curiosity, adaptability, and continuous improvement. UX design is as much about your perspective as it is about your skills. By fostering a user-centered, collaborative, and growth-oriented mindset, you'll be well-prepared to create impactful designs that improve people's lives and enhance their interactions with technology.

Whether you're at the beginning of your journey or already have some experience, remember that a UX career is a path of ongoing learning. Embrace each project, challenge, and lesson as an opportunity to grow, refine your approach, and make a meaningful impact on the user experience. With the right mindset, you'll be equipped to thrive and adapt in a field where creativity, empathy, and innovation are key to success.

Part 2

The Design Thinking Process for UX Beginners

Chapter 4

Introduction to Design Thinking

A User-Centered Approach

Design Thinking is more than just a process; it's a mindset that revolves around empathy, creativity, and a relentless focus on the user. This user-centered approach allows designers to solve complex problems in innovative ways by understanding the people they're designing for. In UX design, Design Thinking helps us frame problems from the user's perspective, ideate with creativity, and develop solutions that are practical and impactful.

In this chapter, we'll delve into what Design Thinking is, why it's valuable in UX design, and how it guides each phase of the design process.

What is Design Thinking?
Design Thinking is a structured, iterative process for creative problem-solving that puts the user at the center. Originally popularized by IDEO and the Stanford d.school, Design Thinking has become a

staple across industries to address various challenges, from product design to organizational strategy.

The core of Design Thinking involves five stages:
1. **Empathize** – Understand the user and their needs.
2. **Define** – Clearly articulate the problem you're solving.
3. **Ideate** – Generate a range of creative solutions.
4. **Prototype** – Build representations of the solutions.
5. **Test** – Evaluate the prototypes to refine and improve.

Each of these stages is flexible and iterative; designers often cycle back to previous steps as they gather new insights or test different ideas.

Why Design Thinking Matters in UX

Design Thinking is powerful in UX design because it directly aligns with the goal of creating meaningful and effective user experiences. Here's why it's essential:

- **User-Centered:** By placing users at the core, Design Thinking ensures that solutions meet real needs. This reduces guesswork and

assumptions, allowing designers to make decisions based on genuine insights.
- **Encourages Innovation:** The structured creativity of Design Thinking helps designers think beyond conventional solutions, leading to fresh and innovative ideas.
- **Adaptable and Iterative:** The iterative nature of Design Thinking means designers can continuously improve and refine their solutions based on user feedback, ensuring the final product truly resonates with users.
- **Reduces Risk:** By testing and prototyping ideas early, designers can identify potential flaws or gaps before they invest significant resources, saving time and reducing development costs.

Using Design Thinking in UX empowers designers to create solutions that are effective, functional, and impactful.

Stage 1: Empathize – Understanding the User

Empathy is the foundation of Design Thinking. In this stage, the goal is to immerse yourself in the user's world and gain a deep understanding of their needs, challenges, and motivations. This step often involves:

- **User Interviews** – Conducting one-on-one interviews to hear directly from users about their experiences, needs, and frustrations.
- **Observation** – Observing users as they interact with products or services in their natural environment, which often reveals insights that interviews alone can't capture.
- **Surveys and Questionnaires** – Gathering quantitative data from a larger audience to get a broader perspective on user needs and trends.

By prioritizing empathy, designers set a strong foundation for solutions that resonate with users on a meaningful level.

Stage 2: Define – Articulating the Problem
Once designers understand the user, the next step is to define the problem clearly. This stage involves synthesizing insights from the empathy phase to create a concise problem statement, also known as a **Point of View (POV) statement**.

A well-defined problem statement:

- **Focuses on Users:** The problem statement should center around the user's experience, challenges, or unmet needs.
- **Is Specific and Actionable:** A clear, specific problem is easier to address than a vague one.

For example, instead of saying, "Our app has usability issues," try, "Our users struggle to locate the settings feature in the app."
- **Inspires Ideation:** A good problem statement naturally leads into brainstorming and ideation, motivating the team to think of creative solutions.

The "Define" stage ensures that the team has a shared understanding of the problem, which keeps the design efforts aligned and purposeful.

Stage 3: Ideate – Generating Solutions
In the Ideate phase, designers shift from problem definition to idea generation. This stage is about exploring a wide range of possible solutions, without judgment or limitations. Techniques like brainstorming, mind mapping, and sketching are often used to spark creativity.

Effective ideation:
- **Encourages Quantity Over Quality Initially:** The goal is to generate as many ideas as possible. Even ideas that seem unrealistic can spark other, more practical solutions.
- **Builds on Each Other's Ideas:** Collaboration and open-mindedness are essential here. By building on each other's thoughts, teams often

come up with unexpected and valuable solutions.
- **Pushes Beyond the Obvious:** The first few ideas that come up are often the most conventional. Pushing beyond those initial thoughts leads to innovative solutions.

Ideation energizes the design process, allowing designers to dream big and think outside the box before refining their ideas.

Stage 4: Prototype – Bringing Ideas to Life
Once the team has some promising ideas, it's time to turn them into tangible prototypes. A prototype is an early model or simulation of the final product, and it doesn't have to be perfect or high-fidelity. The purpose of prototyping is to quickly bring ideas to life so they can be tested and evaluated.

Different forms of prototypes include:
- **Low-Fidelity Prototypes:** Simple sketches, wireframes, or paper models that provide a rough outline of the design.
- **High-Fidelity Prototypes:** More detailed models, often created with tools like Figma, Adobe XD, or Sketch, that resemble the final product more closely.

- **Interactive Prototypes:** Prototypes that users can interact with to simulate the real experience, allowing designers to test functionality and flow.

Prototyping allows designers to visualize solutions, refine them based on practical insights, and prepare them for real user testing.

Stage 5: Test – Evaluating and Refining the Prototype

Testing is the final step in the Design Thinking process, where designers put their prototypes in front of users for feedback. The purpose of testing is to evaluate the effectiveness of the design, identify any issues, and make improvements based on user input.

During testing, designers should:
- **Observe User Reactions:** How users interact with the prototype can reveal unexpected insights that weren't obvious during the ideation or prototyping stages.
- **Ask Targeted Questions:** Encourage users to think out loud as they interact with the design, providing valuable feedback on their experience.
- **Iterate Based on Feedback:** Testing is not a one-time process. After gathering feedback, designers often return to previous

stages—redefining the problem, ideating new solutions, or revising the prototype.

Testing provides critical validation of the design, ensuring it meets user needs before moving forward with development.

The Iterative Nature of Design Thinking
An essential aspect of Design Thinking is that it's non-linear and iterative. Designers often revisit earlier stages as new insights emerge, whether that means returning to user research, redefining the problem, or brainstorming alternative solutions. This flexibility is what makes Design Thinking so effective—it evolves alongside the project, ensuring that the end product aligns with real user needs.

Design Thinking empowers designers to create solutions that are not only functional but meaningful and user-focused. By following this user-centered approach, you'll develop products that not only meet practical requirements but also resonate deeply with users.

As you apply Design Thinking to your UX projects, remember that it's not about following a strict formula but embracing a mindset of empathy, creativity, and iteration. Each stage, from empathy to testing, brings you closer to a solution that enriches the user experience and drives value for both users and stakeholders.

Chapter 5

User Research Fundamentals

Techniques for Understanding Users

User research is the foundation of UX design, enabling designers to make informed decisions that resonate with real users rather than relying on assumptions or guesswork. Effective user research helps you uncover user needs, pain points, and behaviors, guiding the creation of products that are intuitive and impactful. This chapter introduces fundamental user research techniques—interviews, surveys, and personas—and explains how they contribute to a user-centered design process.

Why User Research Matters

User research ensures that your design choices align with the people who will be using the product. It prevents the risks associated with designing in isolation, where personal biases or assumptions can lead to misaligned solutions. When you understand your users well, you're better equipped to create experiences that feel natural, address genuine needs, and add value to their lives.

User research answers critical questions such as:

- Who are our users?
- What are their needs, motivations, and challenges?
- How do they interact with similar products or services?
- What factors influence their decisions?

With clear insights, UX designers can make evidence-based decisions, improving usability, functionality, and satisfaction.

Core User Research Techniques
Let's look at three core techniques for understanding users: interviews, surveys, and personas. Each of these methods provides unique insights and can be adapted to fit the goals of your project.

1. Interviews: Diving Deep into User Experiences
User interviews are a qualitative research technique where you speak directly with users to gather in-depth insights into their thoughts, behaviors, and needs. Through one-on-one conversations, interviews help you uncover the "why" behind user actions, providing a richer understanding of their motivations and pain points.

Key Benefits of Interviews:
- **Detailed Feedback:** Interviews provide nuanced, detailed responses that can reveal underlying motivations and emotions.
- **Uncovering Pain Points:** Users often share specific challenges or frustrations that might not surface in other research methods.
- **Flexibility:** You can ask follow-up questions to clarify responses or explore interesting topics that arise.

Conducting Effective User Interviews:

To conduct valuable user interviews, start by identifying your objectives—what specific insights do you need to gather? Then, create a list of open-ended questions that encourage users to share their experiences, thoughts, and feelings. Here are some best practices:

- **Build Rapport:** Begin with light questions to make users feel comfortable.
- **Ask Open-Ended Questions:** Use questions that start with "How" or "Why" to encourage users to elaborate.
- **Avoid Leading Questions:** Keep questions neutral to avoid influencing users' responses.
- **Listen Actively:** Allow users to speak freely, and avoid interrupting them.

Sample Questions for User Interviews:

- "Can you walk me through how you currently use [product]?"
- "What challenges do you face while using [feature]?"
- "Is there anything you wish you could change about your experience?"

2. Surveys: Gathering Quantitative Data at Scale

Surveys are a quantitative research method used to collect responses from a large audience. They're ideal for validating trends or gaining broad insights into user preferences, behaviors, or demographics. While surveys lack the depth of interviews, they're efficient for gathering data from many users quickly.

Key Benefits of Surveys:

- **Scalability:** Surveys can reach many people at once, making them useful for identifying trends across a large user base.
- **Cost-Effectiveness:** Compared to interviews, surveys are usually quicker and less resource-intensive.

- **Quantitative Insights:** Surveys yield data that can be statistically analyzed to draw patterns and support decision-making.

Creating Effective Surveys:
To design an effective survey, focus on clarity, brevity, and relevance. Only ask questions that serve your research objectives and keep your language clear and straightforward. Here are a few tips:

- **Use Simple Language:** Avoid jargon or complex terms that could confuse respondents.
- **Balance Question Types:** Use a mix of multiple-choice, rating scales, and open-ended questions to gather diverse insights.
- **Avoid Survey Fatigue:** Keep surveys concise. Aim for 10-15 questions to maintain engagement.
- **Pilot Your Survey:** Test the survey with a small group to catch any confusing or ambiguous questions.

Sample Questions for Surveys:

- "How often do you use [feature] in the app?"
- "On a scale of 1-10, how satisfied are you with [product]?"
- "What's the primary reason you use [service]?"

3. Personas: Creating User Profiles to Guide Design

Personas are fictional but data-informed representations of target users. Based on user research, personas help designers understand the needs, motivations, and behaviors of various user segments, ensuring that design decisions resonate with the intended audience. Personas create a shared understanding of who your users are, making it easier to create user-centered experiences.

Key Benefits of Personas:

- **Empathy-Building:** Personas humanize data, allowing designers to empathize with users rather than seeing them as abstract numbers or statistics.
- **Focus and Alignment:** Personas help teams stay focused on user needs, guiding design decisions and preventing feature creep.
- **Communication Tool:** Personas communicate user insights across the team, ensuring everyone has a common understanding of who they're designing for.

Creating Effective Personas:

A persona is crafted using insights gathered from interviews, surveys, and other research. Each persona typically includes demographic details, behaviors, goals, pain points, and a short bio. Here's a breakdown of what a useful persona might include:

1. **Name and Background:** Give your persona a realistic name and basic background information (age, occupation, education).
2. **Demographics:** Include details such as age, gender, location, income, and family status.
3. **Goals and Motivations:** Outline what drives this user's behavior, such as convenience, cost savings, or personal growth.
4. **Frustrations and Pain Points:** List the challenges or obstacles this user experiences that the product can address.
5. **Behavioral Insights:** Describe the user's habits, preferences, and interaction patterns with similar products.

Example Persona:

Name: Sarah Thompson
Age: 34
Occupation: Freelance graphic designer
Location: New York City

Goals: Sarah wants a design tool that integrates well with her current software and helps streamline her workflow.

Pain Points: She finds it frustrating when new tools require a long learning curve. She also values flexibility in her tools since she often juggles multiple projects.

Behavioral Insights: Sarah primarily works from her home office, values convenience, and looks for tools that can support her remote and freelance lifestyle.

By referring to Sarah's persona, designers can stay focused on addressing her specific needs, making it easier to create features and experiences that genuinely resonate with users like her.

Using These Techniques Together
Each research method provides different types of insights that are valuable at various stages of the design process:

- **Interviews** offer deep, qualitative insights that help you understand the "why" behind user behavior.
- **Surveys** give quantitative data that allows you to identify trends and validate assumptions across a broader audience.

- **Personas** synthesize research findings into relatable profiles, helping guide design decisions and keep the team user-focused.

Together, these techniques give you a comprehensive understanding of your users, combining depth with breadth. By leveraging interviews, surveys, and personas, you'll be well-equipped to make user-centered design decisions that enhance usability, functionality, and satisfaction.

User research is at the heart of effective UX design. The insights gathered through interviews, surveys, and personas empower designers to create solutions that resonate with users, improve usability, and drive meaningful engagement. By consistently applying these techniques, you'll develop a clearer understanding of your audience and be better prepared to design experiences that truly meet their needs. Remember, user research is an ongoing process that doesn't end once the design is finalized. Continuous learning and adaptation are essential as user needs evolve and change.

Chapter 6

Step 1 - Empathize with the User

Understanding Needs and Pain Points
Empathy is the foundation of user-centered design. It's the process of seeing the world from the user's perspective, understanding their needs, and recognizing their challenges. In the first step of the design thinking process, "Empathize," designers immerse themselves in the user's world to build a deeper understanding of their experiences. This empathy-driven approach ensures that the solutions we create genuinely address user pain points and meet their needs.

Why Empathy is Essential in UX Design
Empathy enables designers to go beyond assumptions and delve into the real motivations and frustrations users encounter. By truly understanding users, designers can make informed decisions that align with users' goals, creating products that are not only functional but also meaningful and impactful.

Key reasons why empathy is crucial in UX design include:

1. **Creating Relevance**: When we empathize, we design with a user's true needs and values in mind, ensuring that solutions are relevant and valuable.
2. **Uncovering Hidden Pain Points**: Empathy reveals insights that are often overlooked, identifying issues that might not surface in a superficial analysis.
3. **Building Trust and Connection**: Empathetic design leads to experiences that resonate emotionally with users, fostering trust and loyalty.
4. **Encouraging Innovation**: Understanding user challenges can inspire unique solutions that address needs in creative, unexpected ways.

Empathy Techniques for UX Designers
To build empathy with users, designers can utilize various research techniques. Here are three core methods that allow designers to step into the user's shoes and gain meaningful insights: **user interviews**, **shadowing**, and **user journey mapping**.

1. User Interviews: Listening to Users' Stories

User interviews are one of the most powerful ways to develop empathy. By speaking directly with users, designers can explore their thoughts, motivations, and experiences. Interviews provide in-depth information that helps uncover the underlying "why" behind user behaviors.

Best Practices for Conducting Empathetic User Interviews:

- **Start with Open-Ended Questions**: Encourage users to share their experiences by using questions that require more than a "yes" or "no" answer. For example: "Can you describe a recent experience you had with [product]?"
- **Listen Actively**: Allow users to talk freely without interruptions. Nod, ask follow-up questions, and show genuine interest in their responses.
- **Observe Nonverbal Cues**: Pay attention to body language, tone, and facial expressions. These subtle cues can provide additional insights into the user's feelings.
- **Dig Deeper**: Don't settle for surface-level answers. If a user mentions a frustration, ask them to elaborate or give specific examples.

Through user interviews, designers can gain firsthand insight into what users genuinely think and feel about a product, what frustrates them, and what features they wish existed.

2. Shadowing: Observing Users in Their Natural Environment

Shadowing is the practice of observing users as they interact with a product or perform a relevant task in their natural environment. This technique helps designers witness real-world user behavior, revealing pain points, workarounds, and preferences that might not emerge in interviews.

Steps for Effective Shadowing:

- **Clarify Objectives**: Determine what you aim to learn from the shadowing session. For instance, are you observing how users interact with a particular app feature, or are you looking to understand the entire user journey?
- **Blend In**: Try to be as unobtrusive as possible to avoid influencing user behavior. Observe from a distance if possible, letting users engage naturally with the product.
- **Take Notes**: Record your observations carefully, noting each step the user takes and any obstacles or frustrations they encounter.

- **Ask Follow-Up Questions**: After the observation session, ask users to explain certain actions or workarounds you witnessed. This can clarify why users behave the way they do.

Shadowing enables designers to understand the practical aspects of user interaction and identify areas for improvement that may not be obvious in controlled settings.

3. User Journey Mapping: Visualizing the User Experience

A user journey map is a visual representation of the user's experience with a product or service, from start to finish. By mapping out each step of the journey, designers can pinpoint specific moments when users experience challenges, confusion, or delight.

How to Create an Effective User Journey Map:

1. **Define the User's Goal**: Start by identifying what the user wants to achieve. Are they looking to complete a task, find information, or make a purchase?
2. **Outline Each Touchpoint**: Break down each step of the user's journey, from initial interaction to goal completion. Include all

possible touchpoints, such as logging in, navigating features, or receiving support.
3. **Identify Pain Points and Emotions**: At each step, note any challenges the user may face and how these moments make them feel. Frustration, confusion, or satisfaction should be clearly marked.
4. **Look for Opportunities**: Use the journey map to find areas where the experience can be improved. Look for moments when users encounter obstacles, experience delays, or drop off entirely.

User journey mapping helps teams gain a bird's-eye view of the user experience, allowing them to focus on the steps that have the most impact on satisfaction and success.

Building Empathy-Driven Insights
Once empathy research is complete, it's essential to analyze and synthesize the findings. This process turns raw insights into actionable information that can inform the design process.

Methods to Turn Empathy Research into Design Insights:

- **Affinity Mapping**: Organize insights into categories or themes to identify patterns and key takeaways.
- **Problem Statements**: Craft clear statements that describe the user's main challenges, focusing on specific pain points and needs.
- **User Needs and Goals**: List the core needs that emerged from the research, along with any specific goals users expressed.
- **Personas and Empathy Maps**: Use personas and empathy maps to humanize your findings and keep user needs at the forefront during the design process.

By documenting insights clearly, you ensure they are accessible and useful for the entire design team, helping everyone maintain a user-centered perspective throughout the project.

Examples of Empathy in Action

1. **Airbnb**: Early on, Airbnb's founders spent time with hosts to understand their concerns and needs. They discovered that hosts worried about trust and safety when inviting strangers into their homes. This empathy-driven insight led to

features like verified profiles, user reviews, and Airbnb's support services.

2. **Spotify**: Spotify uses empathy research to understand listeners' moods, preferences, and daily routines. This approach led to popular features like personalized playlists and mood-based browsing options, making it easy for users to find music that fits their lives.

Final Thoughts on Empathy in UX Design

Empathy is a skill that grows with practice and dedication. By continuously putting yourself in the user's shoes, you'll deepen your understanding of their world, challenges, and needs. Empathy makes your designs more meaningful and helps you create products that users genuinely value.

This first step in the design thinking process isn't a one-time task; it's an approach to every stage of design. Keep engaging with users, refining your understanding, and applying insights to guide decisions. Empathy will not only make you a better designer but also ensure that your work truly impacts the people it's intended to serve.

Chapter 7

Step 2 - Define the Problem

Identifying Opportunities for Design
After building empathy with users and deeply understanding their needs and challenges, the next step in the design thinking process is to define the problem. In this stage, designers take the insights gathered during the empathize phase and translate them into clear, actionable problem statements. This helps the design team maintain focus on creating solutions that directly address user needs, rather than designing features that may not effectively solve the core issues.

The Importance of Defining the Problem
Defining the problem is about clarity and precision. Without a well-defined problem, it's easy for design projects to go off track, with teams focusing on symptoms rather than the root cause of user frustrations. A clearly articulated problem statement keeps the project grounded and user-centered, guiding the design team toward meaningful solutions.

Key benefits of defining the problem include:

1. **Focusing Design Efforts**: With a clear problem statement, designers can concentrate on areas that will have the greatest impact on user experience.
2. **Avoiding Assumptions**: Defining the problem based on real insights prevents the team from making unfounded assumptions about what users need.
3. **Aligning the Team**: A well-defined problem aligns everyone on the design team, fostering collaboration and ensuring that everyone is working toward the same goal.
4. **Inspiring Innovation**: When the problem is framed effectively, it opens up creative possibilities, encouraging the team to explore innovative solutions.

Creating a Problem Statement

A good problem statement is concise, user-centered, and specific. It articulates the core issue without dictating a solution, allowing room for creative exploration in later steps. The statement should focus on user needs and clearly define what is causing frustration or inefficiency.

Characteristics of an Effective Problem Statement:

- **User-Centered**: The statement should reflect the user's perspective and needs, rather than focusing on business or technical constraints.
- **Broad Enough for Exploration, but Specific Enough to Guide**: The statement should be open-ended, allowing for various potential solutions, yet clear and specific to keep the design focused.
- **Insight-Driven**: Base the statement on real data and insights gathered during the empathy phase, rather than assumptions or guesses.

Example Problem Statement Structure:
[User or persona] needs a way to [user's goal] because [insight or pain point revealed during empathy research].

Example Problem Statements:
1. **For a Food Delivery App**: "Busy urban professionals need a way to order meals quickly during lunch hours because long wait times and unclear delivery estimates are causing frustration and missed lunch breaks."
2. **For a Fitness Tracking App**: "Health-conscious users want a way to see their weekly fitness progress in one glance because

tracking multiple metrics across different screens is time-consuming and overwhelming."
3. **For a Subscription Service**: "Subscribers need an easy way to manage and pause their memberships because complicated cancellation policies lead to frustration and loss of trust."

Defining Design Opportunities

Once the problem statement is in place, the next step is to identify specific opportunities for design within the problem area. This is where designers can start thinking creatively about potential approaches without jumping to final solutions. Identifying design opportunities means breaking down the problem statement into actionable parts that can inspire targeted, innovative ideas.

Steps to Identify Design Opportunities:
1. **Analyze the Problem Statement**: Break down the statement into its core components, focusing on user needs, pain points, and limitations.
2. **Look for Gaps**: Identify any gaps between what users want and what they currently experience. For example, if users want a streamlined process, is there a step that could be simplified or automated?
3. **Ask "How Might We" Questions**: Framing potential solutions as "How might we…"

questions helps open up creative thinking. For example, "How might we reduce wait times?" or "How might we help users find relevant content faster?"
4. **Prioritize Opportunities**: Consider which design opportunities are most feasible and likely to impact user experience. Prioritizing helps the team focus on the solutions that will bring the most value.

Using Personas to Define and Refine the Problem

Personas, which are fictional yet research-based profiles of typical users, are valuable tools in defining the problem. They help keep the problem grounded in real user needs and make it easier to understand how different user types might experience the same issue. By referencing personas during the problem definition phase, designers can clarify the problem and create statements that resonate with diverse user groups.

For example, if you have a persona named "Sarah," a working parent who needs efficient grocery delivery, you can frame the problem with her specific needs in mind. Sarah's busy schedule means she values speed, simplicity, and clear communication around delivery times. This persona-driven approach ensures the problem definition remains relevant and user-centered.

Examples of Problem Definition in Action
Let's explore a couple of real-world examples to see how problem definition can shape the design process:

1. **Dropbox**: In its early days, Dropbox identified a clear problem: people were struggling to access and share files across devices. This problem was specific (file access and sharing), user-centered (focused on people's need for simplicity), and based on actual frustrations. Dropbox's solution—a simple, cross-device file storage service—was a direct response to this defined problem and has become a fundamental tool for millions.
2. **Airbnb**: Before Airbnb existed, travelers had limited options for affordable, unique accommodations. Traditional hotels didn't meet the needs of many travelers who wanted local, authentic experiences. By defining this problem, Airbnb saw a design opportunity to create a platform for people to rent out their homes, offering travelers unique options and local hosts a way to make extra income.
3. **Netflix**: Netflix recognized that users often struggled to find movies they wanted to watch

due to an overwhelming amount of content. The problem definition led to the introduction of personalized recommendation algorithms that prioritize content based on individual viewing preferences. By addressing this problem, Netflix improved the user experience and encouraged longer viewing sessions.

Crafting Design Goals from Problem Statements
With a well-defined problem, the next step is to establish specific design goals. These goals will guide the ideation phase and help ensure that proposed solutions remain focused on addressing user needs. Design goals are measurable and outcome-oriented, helping the team stay on track as they brainstorm and create prototypes.

Examples of Design Goals:

- **Reduce the Time to Complete a Task**: For example, if users find ordering a meal takes too long, the goal might be to reduce the average ordering time by 30%.
- **Enhance User Confidence**: If users feel uncertain about information accuracy, the goal could be to increase user trust by 20% through clearer messaging or feedback mechanisms.
- **Improve Engagement Rates**: If the problem is low interaction, the goal might be to increase

the click-through rate on relevant content by a certain percentage.

Design goals provide clear criteria for success, ensuring that the team has specific outcomes to aim for and can measure the effectiveness of their solutions in the later stages.

The "Define" stage is where empathy meets structure. By translating user insights into clear problem statements and identifying design opportunities, you lay the groundwork for meaningful solutions. A well-defined problem sets the stage for innovation and keeps the project focused on what matters most to the user.

Through careful problem definition, designers create a focused framework that drives purposeful, user-centered solutions.

Chapter 8

Step 3 - Ideate and Brainstorm Solutions

Creative Problem-Solving

After defining a clear and actionable problem statement, it's time to brainstorm creative solutions. The ideation phase is where designers unleash their creativity and explore a wide range of ideas to address the problem. This stage is essential in the design thinking process because it encourages innovation, risk-taking, and out-of-the-box thinking that can lead to groundbreaking solutions.

The Purpose of Ideation in the Design Thinking Process

Ideation is all about generating ideas without immediate judgment. The goal here is to create a rich pool of potential solutions that can later be refined and tested. Even seemingly "wild" ideas can spark unexpected insights or lead to more practical innovations.

Key purposes of the ideation phase include:

1. **Expanding Possibilities**: Ideation removes boundaries, allowing the team to think beyond conventional solutions and explore new approaches.
2. **Encouraging Collaboration**: Brainstorming in a group setting brings diverse perspectives, which can uncover ideas that individual designers may not have considered.
3. **Building Momentum**: Ideation helps to energize the design process, creating excitement around the possibilities for solving user needs.
4. **Nurturing Innovation**: By embracing both feasible and ambitious ideas, teams create space for innovative solutions that may otherwise be overlooked.

Effective Techniques for Ideation and Brainstorming

There are many structured techniques that can help guide ideation sessions. Here are some of the most effective methods for generating ideas:

1. **Brainstorming**: Brainstorming is one of the most popular ideation techniques and involves generating as many ideas as possible within a set timeframe. The emphasis is on quantity over quality, allowing ideas to flow without criticism.

This method works well in a group setting, as one person's idea can inspire others to think in new directions.
Best Practices:
- Encourage all participants to share their ideas, regardless of how unconventional they may seem.
- Set a time limit to keep the session focused and fast-paced.
- Write down every idea for visibility and later reference.

2. **Mind Mapping**: Mind mapping is a visual brainstorming technique that starts with a central problem and branches out into related ideas. This method helps break down complex problems and reveals connections between different concepts.
Best Practices:
- Start with a central problem or theme in the middle of the page.
- Use branches to connect related ideas, expanding outward as more ideas emerge.
- Explore different paths that might not be obvious at first glance.

3. **Sketching**: Sketching or "rapid prototyping" is a great way to bring abstract ideas to life visually. Even rough sketches can make ideas easier to understand and evaluate, and they can

inspire new directions during the ideation process.

Best Practices:
- Encourage quick, low-fidelity sketches to communicate ideas visually.
- Focus on capturing concepts rather than details.
- Use sketches to initiate discussions, allowing team members to build upon one another's visual ideas.

4. **SCAMPER**: SCAMPER is an acronym for a structured approach to creativity that involves seven prompts to modify and improve existing ideas. The prompts are Substitute, Combine, Adapt, Modify, Put to another use, Eliminate, and Reverse. SCAMPER is a versatile tool that can guide participants through various ways of approaching the problem.

Best Practices:
- Apply each SCAMPER prompt to the problem to explore alternative solutions.
- Use SCAMPER prompts to refine or transform existing ideas.
- Encourage team members to be open to unusual interpretations of the prompts.

5. **Worst Possible Idea**: This technique involves intentionally brainstorming the "worst possible ideas" for solving a problem. Although it may

sound counterintuitive, it helps people let go of their inhibitions and generates laughs, which can lead to genuinely creative ideas.

Best Practices:
- Start by discussing ideas that would make the problem worse or are wildly impractical.
- Discuss what makes these ideas bad—this can lead to insights about what could make a good solution.
- Use the "bad" ideas as a springboard to find real, feasible solutions.

6. **Role Playing and Empathy Exercises**: By putting yourself in the users' shoes and acting out potential scenarios, role playing can offer new insights into how users might interact with a product. This technique is particularly effective for uncovering ideas that might not emerge in a traditional brainstorming setting.

Best Practices:
- Have team members act out typical user interactions with the product.
- Explore different user personas and consider their unique needs.
- Observe and discuss potential friction points that arise during role playing.

Setting the Stage for a Productive Ideation Session

Creating a productive ideation environment requires planning and structure. Here are some tips to get the most out of an ideation session:

- **Define the Scope**: Remind the team of the problem statement and key goals. This ensures the ideas generated are aligned with the project's objectives.
- **Encourage a Judgment-Free Zone**: Create a safe space where participants feel comfortable sharing any and all ideas without fear of criticism.
- **Set Time Limits**: Keep the session focused and prevent it from dragging by setting time limits for each activity or brainstorming method.
- **Capture Everything**: Document every idea, no matter how unconventional. You can filter and prioritize them later, but for now, the goal is to generate options.

Evaluating and Selecting Ideas

Once the team has generated a broad array of ideas, it's time to evaluate them. The goal at this stage is to narrow down the ideas to those that best meet the needs outlined in the problem statement and are most feasible for implementation.

Evaluation Techniques:

1. **Dot Voting**: Give each team member a set number of "votes" (usually in the form of sticky dots) to place on their favorite ideas. This simple method allows for quick, democratic prioritization of ideas.
2. **Feasibility-Impact Matrix**: Plot each idea on a matrix based on its feasibility (ease of implementation) and impact (value to the user). This helps teams identify which ideas are both achievable and valuable.
3. **Group Discussion and Debate**: Engage in a structured discussion to weigh the pros and cons of each idea. Consider the insights gathered during user research and the defined problem statement to guide the conversation.
4. **Affinity Mapping**: Group similar ideas together to identify common themes or patterns. This helps in organizing ideas that may have overlapping concepts, allowing the team to develop comprehensive solutions.

Transforming Ideas into Actionable Concepts

After selecting the most promising ideas, the team can begin to flesh them out into actionable concepts. This involves adding details to each chosen idea, such as potential features, user flows, and early-stage sketches. The goal is to build a foundation that can transition smoothly into the prototyping phase.

Steps to Develop Actionable Concepts:
1. **Outline Key Features**: Identify the primary features and functions that will bring the idea to life.
2. **Create User Stories**: User stories are short narratives that describe how a user might interact with the design. They help clarify what each feature should accomplish.
3. **Map User Flows**: User flows outline the steps a user will take to achieve a goal within the product. This helps identify any potential friction points in the journey.
4. **Gather Early Feedback**: Share these initial concepts with stakeholders or potential users to gain early feedback and refine the ideas further.

Real-World Examples of Ideation Success
1. **Airbnb**: During its early stages, Airbnb's founders brainstormed the idea of connecting homeowners with travelers needing short-term accommodations. What started as a simple idea became a groundbreaking model, largely due to the founders' willingness to explore unconventional solutions.

2. **Apple iPod**: In the ideation phase of the iPod, Apple focused on a problem statement around the cumbersome experience of digital music players. The solution was to create a device with a sleek design and intuitive navigation, making music accessible "in your pocket."
3. **Post-it Notes**: Originally a failed adhesive experiment, 3M engineers brainstormed ways to turn the weak adhesive into a solution for temporary note-taking. This led to the creation of Post-it Notes, now one of the world's most iconic office supplies.

Embracing a Growth Mindset in Ideation

The ideation phase is about more than just generating ideas—it's a mindset of openness, curiosity, and experimentation. Teams that embrace a growth mindset during ideation are more likely to discover unique and effective solutions. Encouraging creative freedom and valuing every contribution can help foster an environment where truly innovative ideas are born.

By the end of this chapter, you should have a clear understanding of how to approach ideation in a structured, yet creative way. With the best ideas in hand, the team will be ready to move on to the next phase: prototyping.

Chapter 9

Step 4 - Prototype Your Design

Bringing Ideas to Life

After brainstorming and selecting the most promising ideas, the next step is to bring these concepts to life through prototyping. Prototyping is the process of creating an interactive, low-fidelity version of a design to test its functionality and gather feedback. This step transforms abstract ideas into tangible designs, allowing teams to visualize how users might interact with the product. Prototypes act as a bridge between ideation and user testing, revealing whether the proposed solutions align with user needs and are practical to implement.

What Is a Prototype?

A prototype is an early sample or model of a product, created to test and refine concepts before the final design phase. Prototypes can vary in fidelity, from rough sketches and wireframes to interactive digital models. The goal is to build a simplified version of the design that includes enough functionality to illustrate the main features and user flows without spending too much time on details.

Types of Prototypes:
1. **Low-Fidelity Prototypes**:
   - Simple and inexpensive, often consisting of paper sketches or basic digital wireframes.
   - Ideal for early testing and rapid iteration to explore multiple design directions.
2. **Mid-Fidelity Prototypes**:
   - Includes more detail and functionality, often created with wireframing tools like Figma or Adobe XD.
   - Allows for user flow testing, with clickable links to simulate navigation between screens.
3. **High-Fidelity Prototypes**:
   - Close to the final design, including refined graphics, animations, and interactive elements.
   - Used for in-depth testing, giving users a near-final experience with realistic interactions.

Why Prototyping Is Essential in UX Design

Prototyping is a crucial stage in UX design for several reasons:

1. **Testing Ideas**: Prototypes allow designers to experiment with ideas and see if they work as intended. This hands-on approach brings clarity to concepts that might be challenging to visualize in static wireframes.
2. **Gathering Feedback**: Prototyping enables early feedback from users and stakeholders, helping to identify potential issues or areas for improvement.
3. **Reducing Costs**: Catching design flaws and usability issues early in the process saves time and money by reducing the need for extensive revisions in later stages.
4. **Improving Communication**: Prototypes help teams communicate design intent more effectively. Stakeholders can experience the design directly, which fosters clearer discussions and quicker decision-making.

The Prototyping Process: From Sketch to Interactive Model

The prototyping process follows several stages, with each stage building on the previous one. This progression ensures that designs evolve thoughtfully and that each iteration brings the product closer to meeting user needs.

Step 1: Create Basic Wireframes
Wireframes are simple, low-fidelity layouts that outline the basic structure of each screen or page. They help organize content, define visual hierarchy, and ensure that core features are properly placed.

Best Practices for Wireframes:
- Keep it simple: Focus on structure and layout rather than details.
- Emphasize functionality: Show where key elements like buttons, navigation menus, and images will be placed.
- Label essential elements: Clearly label each part to convey its purpose (e.g., "Header," "Footer," "Main Content Area").

Step 2: Add Interactivity
Once wireframes are complete, start adding interactivity to create a flow between screens. Tools like Figma, Adobe XD, and Sketch allow designers to create clickable prototypes by linking buttons and icons to the relevant pages. This step gives a realistic sense of navigation, helping designers and users test how the flow feels in action.

Best Practices for Adding Interactivity:
- Map out user flows: Define key user journeys, such as signing up or checking out, and link screens to support these paths.

- Use dummy text and placeholders: At this stage, it's acceptable to use placeholder text and images as long as they don't distract from the navigation.
- Test for smoothness: Click through each interaction to ensure a smooth, logical flow from one screen to the next.

Step 3: Build Mid-Fidelity Prototypes
With the main navigation flow established, mid-fidelity prototypes include more refined elements like typography, colors, and icons to make the screens more visually engaging. The focus remains on usability, and designers still avoid high-detail features such as advanced animations.

Best Practices for Mid-Fidelity Prototypes:
- Focus on consistency: Use consistent styles for buttons, fonts, and spacing across screens.
- Include real user feedback: Incorporate initial feedback to improve usability before moving to high fidelity.

- Document feedback: Note areas of confusion or improvement for consideration in the next iteration.

Step 4: Develop High-Fidelity Prototypes
High-fidelity prototypes closely resemble the final product and include polished visuals, animations, and micro-interactions. These prototypes are ideal for final-stage user testing and stakeholder review, as they provide a realistic user experience.

Best Practices for High-Fidelity Prototypes:
- Use real content: Replace placeholders with real text, images, and user data to create an authentic experience.
- Fine-tune interactions: Refine animations, button effects, and other details that contribute to a smooth, enjoyable user experience.
- Ensure accessibility: Check color contrast, text size, and other accessibility standards to ensure usability for all users.

Tools for Prototyping
There are numerous tools available for creating prototypes, each with its unique strengths. Here are some popular options:

1. **Figma**: Known for its collaborative features, Figma allows real-time editing and sharing, making it ideal for team projects.
2. **Adobe XD**: Offers a range of prototyping and animation features with easy-to-use tools, allowing for both simple and complex prototypes.
3. **Sketch**: A design tool popular for UI/UX design that integrates well with other plugins to extend its functionality.
4. **InVision**: Focuses on creating interactive prototypes and offers various collaboration features for team feedback and sharing.
5. **Axure RP**: A tool often used for complex, interactive prototypes, including more advanced features like dynamic content and conditional logic.

Real-World Prototyping Examples

To better understand the value of prototyping, let's look at a few real-world examples:

1. **Airbnb**: Early in its development, Airbnb's founders used prototyping to test the booking process for both hosts and guests. By building low-fidelity clickable prototypes, they could quickly test and refine each step, ensuring a smooth, user-friendly experience before launching.

2. **Slack**: Slack used iterative prototyping to develop its user interface and navigation flow. By creating prototypes for different features like channel creation and message search, the design team could receive user feedback and continuously improve Slack's usability.
3. **Spotify**: Spotify relies heavily on prototyping to develop its complex interface, allowing users to explore the app's content library, playlists, and recommendations. By prototyping early and often, Spotify ensures that every new feature enhances the user experience.

Best Practices for Effective Prototyping

To make the prototyping process as efficient and productive as possible, consider these best practices:

1. **Start Simple**: Begin with low-fidelity prototypes and gradually increase complexity. This ensures that fundamental usability issues are resolved before moving to high-detail design.
2. **Iterate Based on Feedback**: Testing each prototype and incorporating user feedback helps the design evolve in line with real user needs.
3. **Focus on Core Features First**: Prioritize features that are essential to the user experience and leave minor details for later stages.

4. **Maintain Consistency**: Ensure that design elements, like fonts, colors, and icons, remain consistent across screens to build a cohesive user experience.
5. **Test in Realistic Scenarios**: When possible, test prototypes in environments similar to where users will actually use the product. This provides more reliable feedback on usability and flow.

Prototyping as a Collaborative Effort
Prototyping is most effective when done collaboratively. Engaging stakeholders, team members, and even potential users in the process ensures diverse perspectives and minimizes blind spots. This collaborative approach is beneficial not only for improving the design but also for aligning everyone's understanding of the project goals and user needs.

From Prototype to Product
After refining the prototype based on feedback, the next stage involves developing the final product. By this point, the team should have a clear understanding of what works well and what might need further improvement. The validated prototype serves as a blueprint for the final design, ensuring that the development team can bring it to life accurately and efficiently.

The prototyping stage is essential for building a product that not only looks good but also works seamlessly for users. By investing time in thoughtful prototyping, designers ensure that their solutions are user-centered, functional, and ready to make a positive impact when launched.

In this chapter, you've explored the basics of prototyping, its purpose in the design process, and practical steps for creating effective prototypes. With a well-crafted prototype, you're now prepared for the final stage in the design thinking process: testing and refining the design. In the next chapter, we'll dive into user testing techniques to gather insights and fine-tune your prototype for success.

Chapter 10

Step 5 - Test and Refine the Prototype

Usability Testing and Iteration

After creating a prototype, it's time to validate it through testing and refinement. Usability testing is the process of evaluating how effectively users interact with a prototype, identifying what works well, and discovering areas for improvement. Through this step, designers gather essential feedback, helping them shape a product that not only meets user needs but also provides a seamless experience.

What is Usability Testing?

Usability testing is a core part of user experience design, involving real users who interact with the prototype to perform specific tasks. Observing their interactions and challenges helps designers understand how intuitive the product is and where it may fall short.

Usability Testing Objectives:
1. **Identify Pain Points**: Pinpoint where users struggle, feel frustrated, or get confused.

2. **Evaluate Ease of Use**: Assess if the product is easy to navigate and intuitive.
3. **Verify Functionality**: Confirm that features function as intended and meet user expectations.
4. **Gather User Feedback**: Collect qualitative insights directly from users, often revealing needs or preferences that quantitative data might miss.

Types of Usability Testing:

- **Moderated Testing**: A facilitator guides users through the prototype, asking questions and gathering feedback in real-time.
- **Unmoderated Testing**: Users test the prototype independently, with feedback collected afterward through surveys or recorded sessions.
- **Remote Testing**: Users interact with the product from their location, making it easier to include a diverse, geographically dispersed group.

The Usability Testing Process

1. **Define Goals and Objectives**
   - Set clear goals to understand what you want to learn from the test. Objectives can include checking specific features, testing navigation, or evaluating ease of completing a task.
2. **Develop Testing Scenarios and Tasks**
   - Create realistic scenarios that guide users through tasks they would perform using the product. Tasks should reflect common use cases, such as finding a specific feature, completing a transaction, or locating information.
3. **Recruit Participants**
   - Choose participants who represent your target audience to get relevant feedback. Aim for a diverse group to capture a range of perspectives and identify any usability issues that may impact specific user groups.
4. **Conduct the Test**
   - Facilitate the test by encouraging participants to think aloud as they navigate the prototype. This approach helps you understand their thought process and pinpoint why certain aspects may be confusing.

5. **Gather and Analyze Data**
    - After each test, compile findings to identify patterns in user behavior and areas for improvement. Look for issues that multiple users encountered, as these are often high-priority areas to address.

Common Usability Issues to Look For
During usability testing, designers often encounter common issues that may hinder the user experience. Here are some frequent challenges:

1. **Unintuitive Navigation**: Users may struggle to find essential features or paths.
2. **Inconsistent Design Elements**: Variability in buttons, colors, or fonts can confuse users and make the product feel unpolished.
3. **Overloaded Information**: Too much text, complex visuals, or a crowded layout can overwhelm users and decrease usability.
4. **Technical Glitches**: Slow loading times, broken links, or lagging interactions disrupt the experience.
5. **Unclear Instructions**: Instructions that lack clarity can leave users uncertain of how to proceed.

Identifying these issues early through usability testing can help designers refine the prototype, improving its usability and ensuring a smoother experience.

Iterating Based on User Feedback
Testing is not a one-time process; instead, it's a cycle of gathering insights and refining the design. After analyzing usability test results, prioritize the changes based on the impact each issue has on user experience.

Steps for Effective Iteration:
1. **Prioritize High-Impact Changes**: Address major usability issues first, especially those that significantly hinder the user's ability to complete tasks.
2. **Refine the Prototype**: Make changes to the design based on feedback. For example, if users found a button hard to locate, improve its visibility by changing its size, color, or position.
3. **Test Again**: After refining the prototype, test it with another group of users to see if the changes have resolved previous issues and to identify any new ones.
4. **Repeat as Needed**: Continue testing and iterating until the prototype provides a smooth, intuitive experience.

Tools for Usability Testing and Iteration
Several tools make usability testing easier and provide valuable insights, helping you refine your prototype effectively. Here are a few popular options:

1. **UsabilityHub**: Provides a platform for running tests like preference tests and navigation tests.
2. **Lookback**: Offers real-time, moderated testing and session recording, allowing for a detailed analysis.
3. **Maze**: A testing tool that integrates with Figma and Sketch, enabling quick feedback on interactive prototypes.
4. **Hotjar**: Provides heatmaps and session recordings, helping to visualize where users click, scroll, or hesitate.

Iterating for a User-Centered Design
Iteration is essential for creating a truly user-centered product. Each round of testing provides an opportunity to address weaknesses and enhance strengths, moving the design closer to fulfilling user needs and expectations.

Through multiple rounds of testing and refining, designers can create a product that not only functions well but also feels intuitive, engaging, and satisfying for users. This iterative approach ensures that each design decision is informed by real user feedback, making the final product both effective and enjoyable.

In this chapter, you've learned the essentials of usability testing and the importance of iterative refinement in UX design. These steps bring your prototype closer to a final product, ensuring it aligns with user expectations and performs well in real-world scenarios.

Part 3

Essential UX Design Principles and Best Practices

Chapter 11

Core UX Design Principles Every Beginner Should Know (Usability, Accessibility, Visual Hierarchy)

As a UX designer, the principles you apply to your work set the foundation for creating intuitive and enjoyable experiences. Although design is a blend of creativity and functionality, certain core principles guide UX designers to meet user needs effectively. Three of the most crucial principles in UX design are usability, accessibility, and visual hierarchy. Mastering these will equip you to create designs that are not only visually appealing but also intuitive, inclusive, and impactful.

1. Usability: Making Design Intuitive and Easy to Use

Usability is the foundation of any successful user experience. It refers to how effectively, efficiently, and satisfactorily users can complete tasks within a product. An easy-to-use design allows users to navigate without frustration, fostering positive interactions that encourage continued use.

Key Usability Elements:
- **Consistency**: Consistent layouts, fonts, and actions help users predict what will happen when they interact with different parts of your design. Consistency minimizes confusion and builds a sense of familiarity.
- **Feedback**: Immediate feedback lets users know if an action was successful or if there was an error. For example, after submitting a form, a "success" message confirms completion, while a visible error prompt provides clear guidance on any issues.
- **Error Prevention and Recovery**: Effective design anticipates possible mistakes and either prevents them or provides easy ways to fix them. Undo options or clear prompts can prevent users from feeling trapped by their actions.
- **Efficiency**: An efficient design allows users to complete their tasks quickly without unnecessary steps. Streamlining user journeys by simplifying forms or grouping related options can greatly enhance usability.

Tips to Improve Usability:
- Test with real users to see where they struggle.
- Minimize the number of steps needed to accomplish a task.
- Use clear, descriptive labels and instructions to prevent user error.

2. Accessibility: Designing for All Users

Accessibility in UX means creating products that everyone can use, regardless of physical or cognitive ability. Accessible design is not only ethical but also broadens your potential user base. Accessible features benefit users with disabilities while also enhancing usability for everyone.

Core Accessibility Considerations:
- **Color and Contrast**: People with color blindness or low vision may have difficulty distinguishing certain colors. Ensure that text contrasts well against its background and avoid using color alone to convey meaning.
- **Text Size and Readability**: Readable text sizes and fonts make content accessible to users with visual impairments. Aim for at least 16px for body text and avoid overly decorative fonts that can be hard to read.
- **Keyboard Navigation**: Some users cannot use a mouse and rely on keyboards. Design your site or app so that all interactive elements can be

navigated using the keyboard alone, and clearly outline elements when they are in focus.
- **Screen Reader Compatibility**: Screen readers read aloud on-screen content, which is crucial for blind users. To enhance compatibility, ensure elements have clear labels and descriptions. Use semantic HTML elements, like <button> for buttons and <h1> for main headings, to help screen readers convey information accurately.

Designing with Accessibility in Mind:
- Use descriptive alt text for images.
- Make sure interactive elements like buttons are large enough to tap easily.
- Regularly test your design with accessibility tools, like screen readers or color contrast checkers.

3. Visual Hierarchy: Guiding the User's Eye

Visual hierarchy is the organization of design elements to guide users' attention to the most important parts of the interface. An effective visual hierarchy helps users quickly understand the layout and easily find what they need. By manipulating size, color, and positioning, designers can make certain elements stand out and control the flow of information.

Key Components of Visual Hierarchy:
- **Size and Scale**: Larger elements naturally draw attention, so use size to emphasize important components like headings, buttons, or key information. For instance, a prominent call-to-action (CTA) button should stand out as larger or bolder than surrounding text.
- **Color and Contrast**: High-contrast colors are more attention-grabbing, so use them to make important elements pop. For example, a bright-colored button against a neutral background is hard to miss, while a muted color is less attention-demanding.
- **Alignment and Grouping**: Grouping related items close together signals to users that they belong to the same category or function, creating order. Aligning text and images creates a cleaner look that enhances readability and understanding.
- **Whitespace (Negative Space)**: Effective use of whitespace, or empty space around elements, provides visual breathing room, reducing clutter and helping key elements stand out. Whitespace directs users' focus and helps convey importance without overwhelming them.

Applying Visual Hierarchy in UX Design:
- Use contrasting colors for CTAs and critical information.
- Establish a clear typographic hierarchy (e.g., headers, sub-headers, body text).
- Maintain whitespace around elements to avoid a crowded interface.

Putting It All Together: Designing with Usability, Accessibility, and Visual Hierarchy

Balancing usability, accessibility, and visual hierarchy allows you to create designs that are not only functional but also inclusive and user-friendly. For example, a form on a website should:

- Be easy to find and simple to complete (usability),
- Work for people using screen readers and keyboard-only navigation (accessibility),
- Emphasize important fields like "Name" or "Email" by using larger text or brighter colors (visual hierarchy).

Each principle reinforces the others: accessible designs are more usable, and strong visual hierarchy often enhances both usability and accessibility. Keeping these principles at the core of your process ensures you create products that serve users well, fostering positive and seamless interactions.

Moving Forward: Building a Foundation of Effective Design

Mastering these principles is crucial for every aspiring UX designer. By focusing on usability, accessibility, and visual hierarchy, you'll be well-prepared to create digital experiences that meet users' needs and exceed their expectations. These principles serve as essential tools in your design toolkit, empowering you to approach each project with empathy, intentionality, and clarity.

Chapter 12

Accessibility in UX: Designing for Everyone

Designing for accessibility is essential in creating user experiences that include everyone, regardless of their physical, cognitive, or situational limitations. Accessibility in UX design is about removing barriers so that people of all abilities can access and interact with your product. Not only does accessible design support inclusivity, but it also ensures compliance with legal standards and expands your audience reach. This chapter will guide you through essential accessibility principles and practical steps to ensure your designs are usable by everyone.

1. Understanding Accessibility in UX
Accessibility in UX refers to designing interfaces that allow people with disabilities to use and navigate products effectively. Disabilities can range from visual, auditory, motor, and cognitive impairments to temporary or situational limitations, like a broken arm or bright sunlight affecting screen visibility. By focusing on accessibility, you create designs that meet the needs

of all users, ensuring they have an equitable experience.

Why Accessibility Matters:
- **Inclusivity**: Making your designs accessible empowers everyone to use and benefit from your product.
- **Expanded Reach**: An accessible design appeals to a broader audience, including the estimated one billion people globally who live with disabilities.
- **Legal Compliance**: Accessibility is often required by law, such as the Americans with Disabilities Act (ADA) in the U.S., which mandates accessible digital products for businesses.

2. Key Accessibility Principles in UX Design

To make a product accessible, designers should adhere to a few core principles. These are aligned with the Web Content Accessibility Guidelines (WCAG), a globally recognized set of guidelines for making digital content accessible.

Perceivable: Users must be able to perceive the content on the screen. This includes making text readable, providing alternatives for non-text content, and ensuring adequate color contrast.

- *Example*: Adding descriptive alt text to images so that screen readers can describe them to visually impaired users.

Operable: Users must be able to navigate and use all parts of the interface, whether by mouse, keyboard, or assistive technologies.

- *Example*: Ensuring all interactive elements, like buttons, can be reached and activated using only the keyboard.

Understandable: Content should be easy to understand, regardless of a user's cognitive ability.

- *Example*: Writing clear, concise instructions for completing a form and avoiding overly complex language.

Robust: The design should work across different devices, browsers, and assistive technologies.

- *Example*: Testing your product with screen readers, such as JAWS or VoiceOver, to ensure compatibility.

3. Key Accessibility Practices for UX Designers

Creating accessible designs requires attention to specific details. Below are practical steps to ensure accessibility in common design scenarios.

Text and Typography
- Use legible fonts and appropriate sizes. Aim for a minimum of 16px for body text.
- Avoid overly decorative fonts, which may be difficult for some users to read.
- Ensure high contrast between text and background. Tools like the WCAG Color Contrast Checker can help confirm you meet accessibility standards.

Color and Contrast
- Don't rely on color alone to convey information. Use labels, icons, or patterns to differentiate elements.
- Ensure sufficient color contrast, especially for text. For instance, black text on a white background or vice versa provides excellent readability.

Images and Media

- Add descriptive *alt text* to images. This text allows screen readers to convey the meaning of the image to visually impaired users.
- Include captions or transcripts for audio and video content, making it accessible for users with hearing impairments.

Interactive Elements and Navigation
- Design buttons, forms, and links that can be easily accessed via keyboard alone. Test each function using only the "Tab" and "Enter" keys to ensure it is fully accessible.
- Provide clear labels on buttons and interactive elements, so users know their purpose. Avoid vague labels like "Click here" and opt for descriptive ones like "Submit" or "Download Report."
- Ensure form inputs are labeled properly, allowing screen readers to interpret and convey the form's purpose clearly.

Layouts and Spacing
- Use sufficient whitespace to prevent clutter, making your design easier to navigate and understand.

- Group related elements together, creating a logical flow that enhances comprehension.

4. Making Accessibility Testing Part of Your Process

Incorporate accessibility checks throughout the design and development process, rather than leaving them as an afterthought. Accessibility testing tools can help identify potential issues before your product reaches users.

Accessibility Testing Tools:
- **Wave**: Provides visual feedback on accessibility issues and helps identify areas needing improvement.
- **Axe**: A browser extension that scans for WCAG compliance and highlights elements that don't meet accessibility standards.
- **Color Contrast Checkers**: These tools ensure your design meets minimum contrast standards.

User Testing for Accessibility: In addition to automated tools, user testing with people who have disabilities can reveal insights that automated tests might miss. This real-world feedback is invaluable for understanding how accessible your design truly is.

5. Accessibility Across Devices and Situations

It's essential to consider accessibility for users across various devices, including desktops, tablets, and mobile devices. Many people also use assistive technologies, like screen readers, text-to-speech software, and braille displays. Ensuring cross-device compatibility makes your product accessible in diverse environments, enhancing usability for everyone.

Responsive Design and Mobile Accessibility:
- Use flexible layouts that adapt to different screen sizes.
- Ensure touch targets are large enough on mobile devices for users with limited dexterity.
- Simplify navigation on smaller screens, as dense menus can be challenging for some users to operate.

6. The Ethical Responsibility of Accessibility

Designing for accessibility is a reflection of empathy and respect for all users. An inclusive design shows your commitment to providing equal access, which is increasingly valued by users and necessary for responsible business practices. Accessibility is not only about meeting standards—it's about prioritizing human-centered design and recognizing the diverse ways users engage with your product.

Ethical Benefits of Accessibility:
- **User Trust**: When users feel that their needs are considered, they are more likely to trust and value your product.
- **Social Responsibility**: Designing for accessibility contributes to a more equitable society, empowering people of all abilities to participate fully in the digital world.

Bringing Accessibility into Your UX Workflow

Making accessibility an integral part of your UX process ensures that inclusivity becomes second nature in your designs. Start by familiarizing yourself with WCAG standards, adopting accessible design practices, and consistently testing your designs with both automated tools and real users. As you gain experience, accessibility will become a natural aspect of your design approach, empowering you to create products that truly serve everyone.

By designing with accessibility in mind, you make a powerful contribution to creating a world where digital experiences are open and inclusive to all. Accessibility is not just a design consideration but a commitment to building a more inclusive digital landscape.

Chapter 13

Case Studies: Lessons from Real UX Projects

Case studies offer invaluable insights into how UX principles and strategies apply in real-world scenarios. Each project has unique challenges, goals, and constraints, providing diverse learning opportunities. In this chapter, we'll explore three case studies from successful UX projects, covering a range of industries, audiences, and design challenges. These examples will highlight how thoughtful UX design not only solves immediate user needs but also contributes to business growth, user satisfaction, and long-term engagement.

Case Study 1: Improving E-commerce User Experience for a Fashion Retailer

Background: An online fashion retailer noticed a high cart abandonment rate and low customer retention, despite strong initial website traffic. The company wanted to redesign the user experience to increase conversions and boost customer loyalty.

Challenge: The existing website was visually appealing but had usability issues that led to frustration, particularly during the checkout process. Users reported confusion navigating product categories, difficulty finding key product information, and a lengthy, cumbersome checkout flow.

UX Approach:

1. **User Research**: The UX team conducted interviews and surveys with both existing and potential customers. They identified key pain points: complex navigation, lack of product filters, and too many steps to complete a purchase.
2. **Persona Development**: Based on research, the team created user personas representing different shopper types—bargain hunters, style-conscious buyers, and busy professionals—each with unique needs and behaviors.
3. **Redesign and Prototyping**: The team streamlined the site navigation and added comprehensive filtering options for faster product searches. They simplified the checkout process, reducing it to three key steps: review cart, payment information, and order confirmation.

4. **Usability Testing**: The prototype was tested with a sample group representing the user personas, and feedback indicated improved ease of use and satisfaction with the changes.

Outcome: After implementing the redesign, the retailer saw a 30% reduction in cart abandonment and a 25% increase in repeat customers. This case highlights the importance of understanding user pain points, designing for simplicity, and continually refining based on user feedback.

Key Lesson: Prioritizing ease of navigation and a streamlined checkout process can directly impact conversion rates and customer retention in e-commerce.

Case Study 2: Redesigning a Health App for Better Engagement and Compliance

Background: A health-tech company created a mobile app to help users manage chronic conditions by tracking symptoms, medication, and lifestyle choices. However, the app struggled with user engagement, and many users abandoned it after the first few uses.

Challenge: Users found the app difficult to navigate, and it failed to provide a sense of progress or motivation. Additionally, the app lacked customization options, making it hard for users with different conditions to find relevant information and tools.

UX Approach:

1. **Empathy Mapping**: To deeply understand users' emotional journeys, the UX team developed empathy maps that reflected users' daily experiences managing their health.
2. **Feature Prioritization**: By identifying the most critical user tasks, such as medication reminders and symptom tracking, the team reduced clutter and streamlined the main dashboard for easy access to essential features.
3. **Gamification Elements**: The team incorporated gamification to encourage regular use, such as a daily streak counter for consistent logging and badges for reaching health milestones.
4. **Accessibility Improvements**: Recognizing that some users might have visual impairments or limited dexterity, the design included larger text options, simplified navigation, and support for screen readers.

Outcome: The redesigned app achieved a 40% increase in daily active users and saw higher engagement with core features like symptom tracking and medication reminders. Users reported feeling more motivated to log their data, and health compliance improved as a result.

Key Lesson: In health-related UX, simplifying task flows, incorporating motivational elements, and ensuring accessibility are vital to sustaining user engagement and improving outcomes.

Case Study 3: Enhancing a Banking App's UX for an Aging Audience

Background: A bank noticed that their mobile app usage was particularly low among senior customers, who reported frustration with the app's complexity. The goal was to make the app more intuitive for elderly users, who are often less tech-savvy and have different accessibility needs.

Challenge: The app had small, dense text, icons that were not universally recognizable, and an overload of features that made navigation overwhelming. Additionally, many users struggled with security features like two-factor authentication (2FA), which were challenging to set up and use.

UX Approach:
1. **User Interviews with Senior Customers**: The UX team held one-on-one interviews with senior customers to understand their specific

needs, concerns, and typical behaviors when using digital banking.

2. **Simplified Navigation and Design**: A "simplified mode" was introduced, featuring larger text, easy-to-read fonts, high-contrast colors, and clear labels. Icons were redesigned for better recognition, and the main dashboard was simplified to show only the most frequently used features (balance check, transfer, and payment).
3. **Streamlined Security**: The team collaborated with developers to introduce a more straightforward authentication method, like biometric login, which eliminated the need for complex password entry.
4. **Accessibility Testing**: The prototype was tested with older users to ensure ease of use and accessibility, and further refinements were made based on their feedback.

Outcome: The bank saw a 50% increase in app usage among customers aged 60 and above, along with a 70% decrease in customer service calls related to app navigation. This positive response demonstrated that designing for accessibility and simplicity could make a dramatic difference in user engagement, especially for older audiences.

Key Lesson: When designing for an aging audience, prioritize clarity, accessibility, and ease of navigation to create a more inclusive, user-friendly experience.

Insights and Takeaways from the Case Studies

These case studies underscore several critical aspects of successful UX design:

- **User-Centered Design**: Every project began with a deep understanding of the users, whether through interviews, personas, or empathy mapping. Knowing the user base is fundamental to delivering a product that genuinely meets their needs.
- **Iterative Testing**: Each case involved prototyping and testing, allowing designers to refine solutions based on real user feedback. This iterative approach helped identify potential pain points early and ensured that final products were user-friendly and effective.
- **Simplicity and Accessibility**: Reducing complexity, prioritizing essential features, and making designs accessible led to better usability across the board. Accessible design not only meets the needs of diverse user groups but often benefits all users.

- **Customization and Personalization**: Providing options that let users customize their experience or display relevant features creates a sense of control and satisfaction, as shown in both the health and banking app redesigns.

Applying Lessons from Real UX Projects to Your Own Work

As you progress in your UX career, draw on the principles seen in these case studies. Emphasize user-centered design, build an understanding of your users through research, and commit to iterative testing. Keep in mind that accessibility, simplicity, and clear navigation are universally beneficial design elements. Even if your audience isn't as specialized as these cases, these principles will guide you in creating intuitive, effective designs that meet real needs.

Case studies like these offer not only insights but also inspiration to tackle UX challenges creatively and empathetically. The more you engage with real-world examples, the better equipped you'll be to approach your projects with practical strategies that lead to meaningful, impactful design.

Part 4

Developing Practical Skills and Building Your Portfolio

Chapter 14

Effective Communication in UX Design: Visual and Verbal Skills

Communication is at the heart of UX design. As a UX designer, your role is to bridge the gap between users and technology, creating an experience that feels natural and intuitive. This requires more than just technical skills; it demands an ability to communicate effectively both visually and verbally. In this chapter, we'll explore the importance of these skills and how you can apply them to convey ideas, collaborate with teams, and design user experiences that speak directly to the needs of your audience.

1. The Role of Visual Communication in UX Design
Visual communication in UX is about guiding users through an experience in a way that feels natural and effortless. By mastering visual hierarchy, balance, and flow, you ensure that users can

understand information quickly, make decisions confidently, and navigate seamlessly.

Key Aspects of Visual Communication:

- **Hierarchy and Layout**: Visual hierarchy is the arrangement of elements to show their order of importance. For instance, larger or bolder elements catch the user's attention first. Effective layout directs the user's gaze in a way that aligns with their goals, making it easy for them to find what they need without feeling overwhelmed.
- **Consistency**: Consistency in design—whether in fonts, colors, or layout—helps users recognize patterns and navigate more efficiently. When users encounter consistent design elements, they understand intuitively what actions to take, reducing cognitive load.
- **Simplicity**: Visual clarity is essential. Removing unnecessary elements from a design prevents clutter, allowing the focus to remain on what matters most. Good UX design emphasizes simplicity to make interaction straightforward and satisfying.

2. Verbal Communication: Conveying Ideas with Clarity

Verbal communication is equally critical in UX design. Whether you're explaining your ideas to a team or creating text within the user interface, clarity and precision are paramount. Effective verbal communication makes users feel understood and provides them with essential guidance.

Key Aspects of Verbal Communication:

- **Clear and Concise Language**: Users don't want to wade through complex jargon. When writing for interfaces, labels, or instructions, always prioritize clarity. Use simple, direct language that matches the user's own vocabulary.
- **Tone and Voice**: The tone and voice in UX writing help build a connection with users. For example, a banking app might adopt a professional and reassuring tone, while a fitness app may choose a more upbeat and motivating voice. Tailoring your tone builds trust and reinforces brand identity.
- **Microcopy**: Microcopy refers to the small bits of text that guide users through an interface, such as button labels, error messages, and tooltips. Well-crafted microcopy can prevent

user errors, clarify actions, and even make the experience more enjoyable by adding a friendly or helpful tone.

3. Collaboration and Communicating with Teams

UX designers often work as part of a team, which may include developers, product managers, marketing specialists, and stakeholders. Effective communication skills help you convey the rationale behind design choices, gather feedback, and align on project goals.

Strategies for Effective Team Communication:

- **Presenting Your Work**: Explain your design decisions in a way that aligns with business goals and user needs. Share how each element contributes to solving user problems and ask for specific feedback to improve clarity and alignment.
- **Using Visuals to Communicate Ideas**: Wireframes, prototypes, and journey maps are invaluable for explaining your ideas to team members who may not be familiar with design concepts. Visuals help everyone understand the

intended user flow and provide a tangible reference point for feedback.
- **Giving and Receiving Feedback**: Constructive feedback is essential for refining your designs. Be open to input, and always frame feedback in terms of improving the user experience. Similarly, when providing feedback, focus on specific, actionable points rather than general opinions.

4. Communication Skills with Users: The Value of User Feedback

Gathering user feedback is a core aspect of UX design, allowing you to continually refine and enhance the product based on real-world input. Your communication with users should be respectful, open, and genuinely focused on understanding their needs and pain points.

Methods for Effective User Communication:

- **User Interviews and Surveys**: Conducting interviews or surveys with real users provides valuable insights into their experiences. Approach these conversations with empathy, and ask open-ended questions to encourage honest responses.

- **Clear Instructions and Usability Testing**: When testing a prototype, give clear instructions to users on what you would like them to do. Encourage them to think aloud during the process, providing insight into their thought patterns and reactions.
- **Iterating Based on Feedback**: After collecting feedback, identify common themes and pain points that can be addressed in the design. Iterating based on user feedback ensures that your design is grounded in actual user needs, creating a more relevant and effective experience.

5. Practical Tips for Enhancing Communication Skills in UX

Developing effective communication skills is a process, but there are practical ways to strengthen both your visual and verbal abilities:

- **Practice Sketching and Wireframing**: Quick sketches or wireframes are powerful tools for communicating ideas visually. Practice creating wireframes to clarify your design thinking before moving to high-fidelity prototypes.
- **Study UX Writing Principles**: UX writing is a skill that can be honed. Familiarize yourself

with principles of clear, user-friendly writing by analyzing well-designed interfaces and observing how other designers craft their words.
- **Get Comfortable with Presentations**: Public speaking and presentations are part of most design careers. Practice explaining your designs to others in a way that is simple and compelling. Consider joining a public speaking group or attending workshops to build confidence.

Effective communication is the backbone of UX design. By mastering visual and verbal skills, you can create interfaces that are both visually intuitive and verbally clear, guiding users seamlessly through their journey. Your ability to communicate also enhances collaboration, allowing you to bring together diverse perspectives to create a unified design vision. As you refine these skills, you'll find that your designs become not only more user-centered but also more aligned with the goals of everyone involved—from users to stakeholders.

Chapter 15

Building a Compelling UX/UI Portfolio: Showcase Your Work

Your UX/UI portfolio is more than just a showcase of your skills—it's your professional story, a visual resume that communicates who you are as a designer and what unique qualities you bring to the table. Whether you're just starting out in UX/UI or have some experience, a well-crafted portfolio can set you apart in a competitive field. In this chapter, we'll cover the essentials of building a compelling portfolio, including what to include, how to present your work, and tips for making an impactful impression on potential employers and clients.

1. Why a Portfolio Matters

A strong UX/UI portfolio is crucial because it demonstrates your design thinking, problem-solving skills, and creativity in a tangible way. Unlike a resume or LinkedIn profile, your portfolio allows potential employers and clients to directly experience your approach to user-centered design, seeing how you think through challenges and create meaningful solutions.

A great portfolio:

- **Showcases Your Process**: Employers want to see more than final screens or polished visuals—they want to understand how you approached each project, the challenges you faced, and the solutions you created.
- **Demonstrates Your Skills**: A portfolio is an opportunity to highlight a range of skills, including user research, wireframing, prototyping, visual design, and usability testing.
- **Tells Your Story**: A thoughtful portfolio reveals your professional journey, showing how your skills have developed over time and what makes you unique as a designer.

2. Essential Elements of a UX/UI Portfolio

When building your portfolio, focus on these key components to ensure it provides a clear and comprehensive picture of your abilities:

- **Case Studies**: Case studies form the core of any UX/UI portfolio. A well-structured case study should walk the viewer through the full design process, from identifying the problem to researching user needs, creating solutions, and

testing prototypes. Aim to include three to five strong case studies that showcase a variety of projects.
- **Role and Responsibilities**: Clearly outline your role in each project, especially if you worked as part of a team. Specify which aspects of the project you were responsible for, such as user research, visual design, or interaction design.
- **Problem Statement and Goals**: For each case study, begin with a problem statement to explain the project's context and purpose. State the design goals and objectives clearly, which helps viewers understand the direction and focus of your work.
- **Process and Methods**: Detail your design process and the methods you used, such as user interviews, surveys, journey mapping, wireframing, prototyping, and usability testing. This helps potential employers see your approach and commitment to user-centered design.
- **Outcomes and Reflections**: Don't just end with the final design—showcase the results. If possible, include metrics or feedback that demonstrate the effectiveness of your design. Reflect on what you learned and how you might approach things differently in future projects.

3. Structuring a Case Study

A clear, well-organized case study structure makes it easier for viewers to follow your process and understand your work. Here's a common structure for UX/UI case studies:

1. **Introduction**: Briefly introduce the project, the client or organization (if applicable), and the overall design challenge.
2. **Problem Statement**: Describe the user problem you aimed to solve and why it was significant.
3. **Research and Insights**: Summarize your research process, findings, and any insights you gathered from user research.
4. **Ideation and Prototyping**: Show how you generated ideas, refined them, and built prototypes. Include wireframes, sketches, or mockups to illustrate your process.
5. **Design Solution**: Present your final design, with an explanation of how it addresses the problem. Highlight the main features and user flows.
6. **Usability Testing and Iteration**: Describe any testing you conducted and any iterations made based on feedback. Explain how user feedback informed your final design decisions.

7. **Outcome**: Conclude with the results, including metrics (if available), and reflect on what you learned.

4. Choosing the Right Projects

When selecting projects to include, aim for variety and relevance. Choose projects that reflect the type of work you're interested in pursuing. If you're looking for a job in e-commerce design, for example, include projects that demonstrate your experience in building seamless, user-friendly shopping experiences.

Types of Projects to Include:

- **Real-World Projects**: These could be work you completed for clients, internships, or freelance work. Real-world projects show that you can work within constraints and deadlines, producing work that meets actual user and business needs.
- **Personal Projects**: If you're new to UX/UI or want to highlight a particular skill, personal projects can be valuable. These allow you to demonstrate your passion for design and show how you tackle problems independently.
- **Redesigns**: Redesign projects—where you take an existing product or website and reimagine

it—can be a good way to showcase your skills, especially if you don't have much real-world experience.

5. Presenting Your Portfolio: Digital Platforms and Formats

Today, most UX/UI designers opt for digital portfolios, as they're easily accessible and allow for interactive presentation of your work. Common platforms include:

- **Website Portfolios**: Building a personal website using tools like WordPress, Wix, or Squarespace allows for a fully customized portfolio. A personal website also gives you a professional edge and can showcase your visual design skills.
- **Portfolio Platforms**: Platforms like Behance, Dribbble, and Adobe Portfolio offer easy ways to create and share portfolios without the need for coding or extensive setup.
- **PDF Portfolios**: While less interactive, PDF portfolios can still be effective, especially for interviews or as downloadable attachments. Make sure your PDF is well-organized, easy to navigate, and optimized for both desktop and mobile viewing.

6. Design Tips for a Polished Portfolio

An attractive and user-friendly portfolio layout can help your work shine. Here are a few tips for creating a visually appealing portfolio:

- **Consistency**: Maintain a consistent visual style throughout your portfolio. Use the same fonts, colors, and layout structure to create a cohesive look.
- **Emphasize Key Information**: Highlight important details, such as your role, challenges, and outcomes. Use headings, bullet points, and visuals to guide the reader's attention.
- **Use High-Quality Images**: Include crisp, high-resolution images of your designs. If showing digital prototypes or interactive elements, consider using GIFs or video snippets.
- **Less is More**: Avoid clutter. Let each project stand on its own and give it ample space on the page. A clean, minimal layout can make your portfolio look more professional and easier to navigate.

7. Tailoring Your Portfolio for Different Opportunities

Not all opportunities require the same approach to presenting your work. Tailor your portfolio to align with the specific job or client you're pursuing. For example:

- **For Job Applications**: Highlight projects relevant to the role you're applying for. If a position focuses on user research, consider adding extra details about the research methods and insights from your case studies.
- **For Freelance Clients**: Showcase a diverse range of projects to demonstrate versatility. If you have experience working with businesses of different sizes, emphasize that, as it shows adaptability.
- **For Specific Industries**: If you're applying for a role in a specialized industry (e.g., healthcare or e-commerce), include projects related to that field to show your familiarity with industry-specific challenges.

Creating a compelling UX/UI portfolio is an ongoing process, not a one-time task. As you gain more experience and skills, regularly update your portfolio with new projects and refine existing case studies. Think of it as a living document that reflects your growth, showcasing the evolution of your design abilities and professional journey.

A well-crafted portfolio can open doors to new opportunities, serve as a point of pride in your career, and act as a source of inspiration for others in the UX/UI field. As you move forward, let your portfolio be a testament to your dedication to solving real problems, creating meaningful experiences, and continuously learning in the ever-evolving world of UX/UI design.

Chapter 16

Essential Tools and Resources for UX Designers (Research, Wireframing, Prototyping Tools)

The world of UX design is vast, and having the right tools and resources is essential to deliver high-quality, user-centered designs efficiently. From conducting user research to creating detailed prototypes, each stage of the UX process can benefit from specialized tools designed to streamline and enhance your work. In this chapter, we'll cover the essential tools for research, wireframing, and prototyping, along with a few resources to help you stay up-to-date and continuously improve your skills.

1. Research Tools: Understanding the User

User research is the foundation of UX design. It provides the insights that guide design decisions and ensure that products meet the actual needs of users. Effective research tools help designers collect, analyze, and interpret data, allowing for a deeper understanding of user behavior, needs, and pain points.

Popular Research Tools for UX Designers

- **UserTesting**: This platform allows you to conduct remote usability tests by recording real users as they interact with your product. You can ask specific questions, set tasks, and receive detailed feedback, which can be invaluable for understanding user experience at different stages of the design.
- **Dovetail**: Dovetail is a powerful tool for organizing and analyzing qualitative data from user interviews, surveys, and feedback sessions. It's ideal for managing and tagging insights, spotting trends, and building a clear picture of user needs.
- **Google Analytics**: For designers working on digital products, Google Analytics is essential for understanding how users interact with a product over time. By analyzing user behaviors and patterns, designers can identify areas that need improvement and optimize the experience accordingly.
- **Lookback**: Lookback enables live and recorded user testing, interviews, and focus groups, with

options for screen sharing and face-to-face interaction. It's particularly useful for remote user research and collaborative insights gathering.
- **Hotjar**: This tool combines heatmaps, session recordings, and user feedback surveys, making it a great choice for understanding user behavior on websites. It allows you to see where users are clicking, scrolling, or dropping off, helping you to identify usability issues.
- **SurveyMonkey**: For UX designers conducting surveys, SurveyMonkey is a flexible and widely used tool. It enables you to design customized surveys, collect responses, and analyze data, which can be useful for gathering quantitative insights from users.

2. Wireframing Tools: Structuring the Layout

Wireframing is a critical step in the UX process. It allows designers to visualize the layout and functionality of a product before investing time in creating a high-fidelity design. Wireframes serve as blueprints that outline the structure, helping to communicate ideas clearly to stakeholders and team members.

Popular Wireframing Tools for UX Designers

- **Balsamiq**: Balsamiq is a user-friendly tool designed specifically for creating low-fidelity wireframes. It's a favorite among beginners and experienced designers alike, allowing for quick, sketch-like wireframes that focus on structure rather than aesthetics.
- **Sketch**: Sketch is widely used for both wireframing and high-fidelity design, offering powerful features and plugins to streamline workflows. Its intuitive interface and flexible grid system make it easy to design wireframes that can later be converted into high-fidelity mockups.
- **Figma**: Figma is an excellent choice for collaborative wireframing and prototyping. With cloud-based capabilities, it allows teams to work on wireframes in real-time, making it easier to share, review, and iterate with stakeholders.
- **Adobe XD**: Adobe XD combines wireframing, prototyping, and UI design features, offering a complete solution for UX designers. Its user-friendly interface and integration with other Adobe products make it a popular choice for designers already familiar with Adobe's ecosystem.

- **Axure RP**: Known for its advanced functionality, Axure RP is ideal for wireframes that require interactivity and complexity. It allows designers to create detailed, high-fidelity wireframes with built-in interactions, making it useful for projects that demand precise user flows.
- **Wireframe.cc**: This simple, browser-based tool is perfect for quick, low-fidelity wireframes. Its minimalist design and limited features make it easy to focus on the basics of structure and layout without being overwhelmed by options.

3. Prototyping Tools: Bringing Designs to Life

Prototyping transforms static wireframes into interactive models, allowing designers and stakeholders to experience how users might interact with the product. This stage is essential for testing usability, gathering feedback, and making necessary adjustments before development begins.

Popular Prototyping Tools for UX Designers

- **InVision**: InVision is a powerful tool that lets you turn static designs into clickable, interactive prototypes. It's particularly useful for presenting

design flows and transitions, making it easy for stakeholders to visualize the user journey.
- **Figma**: In addition to wireframing, Figma's prototyping features make it a versatile tool for UX designers. It supports interactive components, animated transitions, and easy sharing, allowing for seamless testing and feedback collection.
- **Adobe XD**: Adobe XD's prototyping tools offer a range of features, including voice interaction, animations, and component states. Designers can create sophisticated prototypes and share them for user testing, making it a strong choice for both prototyping and design.
- **Marvel**: Marvel is a beginner-friendly tool that offers wireframing, prototyping, and user testing capabilities. Its simple interface makes it ideal for quickly creating interactive prototypes without a steep learning curve.
- **ProtoPie**: ProtoPie enables designers to create highly interactive prototypes with micro-interactions and advanced animation capabilities. It's ideal for mobile app prototyping, where gestures and transitions are essential for the user experience.
- **Framer**: Framer's advanced prototyping capabilities are geared toward experienced designers who want more control over

animation and interaction. It allows you to create complex, highly interactive prototypes with real code, offering unmatched flexibility.

4. Staying Updated: Learning Resources and Communities

In a rapidly evolving field like UX design, staying updated with the latest tools and practices is crucial. Many online resources and communities offer courses, tutorials, and insights that can help designers continuously improve their skills and stay ahead of trends.

Recommended Learning Resources

- **Interaction Design Foundation (IDF)**: IDF offers affordable, high-quality courses covering various UX topics, from beginner to advanced. Their comprehensive curriculum and expert instructors make it a go-to resource for many designers.
- **Coursera and Udemy**: Both platforms offer UX and UI design courses from top universities and professionals. With topics covering design thinking, usability, and advanced prototyping, they're ideal for learning new skills or deepening existing knowledge.

- **YouTube**: YouTube has a vast library of UX design tutorials, reviews, and case studies. Channels like The Futur, AJ&Smart, and DesignCourse provide valuable insights into UX best practices, tool tutorials, and industry trends.

Popular UX Design Communities

- **Designer Hangout**: A Slack-based community with over 18,000 UX designers worldwide, Designer Hangout offers a space for networking, feedback, and discussion on a range of UX topics.
- **UX Stack Exchange**: This question-and-answer site allows designers to ask questions, share insights, and get advice on specific UX challenges.
- **Dribbble and Behance**: While primarily portfolio platforms, Dribbble and Behance also serve as communities where designers can share their work, gain inspiration, and connect with others in the field.

5. Selecting the Right Tools for Your Workflow

When choosing tools, consider your specific needs, design style, and project requirements. Many UX designers use a combination of tools, selecting those that fit best at each stage of the process. Here are a few tips for finding the right tools:

- **Experiment**: Most tools offer free trials or basic plans, so try different options to see which fit best with your workflow and preferences.
- **Stay Flexible**: As UX design evolves, so do the tools. Don't hesitate to adapt and learn new tools that can enhance your workflow and improve your productivity.
- **Focus on Essentials**: While new tools are exciting, remember that mastering a few core tools is often more valuable than using every available option. Focus on tools that provide value across multiple stages of the design process.

Equipped with the right tools, UX designers can streamline their process, enhance collaboration, and produce impactful, user-centered designs. By mastering essential research, wireframing, and prototyping tools, you can significantly improve both the efficiency and quality of your work. As the UX field continues to grow, new tools and resources will emerge—embrace these advancements, stay curious, and refine your toolkit to keep delivering designs that resonate with users.

Part 5

Preparing for a Successful UX Career

Chapter 17

Creating a Clear UX Career Roadmap: Setting Goals and Objectives

Building a career in UX design can be immensely rewarding, but it requires thoughtful planning and clear goals. A well-defined roadmap helps you navigate your professional growth, stay on track with your development, and achieve your long-term ambitions. In this chapter, we'll cover how to set clear goals, create actionable objectives, and outline practical steps to help you thrive in a UX career.

1. Understanding the Importance of a UX Career Roadmap

A roadmap is more than a list of career aspirations; it's a structured plan that outlines where you want to go and how to get there. A career in UX design offers numerous opportunities and specializations—from research and interaction design to information architecture and usability testing. Knowing what you want to achieve can help you focus on acquiring the specific skills, experiences, and connections you need to succeed.

Why a UX Career Roadmap is Essential:

- **Provides Direction**: With a roadmap, you can pinpoint the skills, knowledge, and experiences necessary for your desired role.
- **Enhances Motivation**: Clear goals keep you motivated, especially when navigating challenges or learning complex skills.
- **Tracks Progress**: A structured roadmap allows you to see how far you've come, helping you stay confident and focused.
- **Facilitates Adaptability**: The UX field evolves rapidly, and a roadmap helps you adapt your goals to stay relevant.

2. Identifying Your Career Goals in UX Design

The first step in creating a career roadmap is to identify your long-term and short-term goals. Start by asking yourself what excites you about UX design and where you see yourself in the future. Here are some examples of goals that aspiring and practicing UX designers might have:

- **Long-Term Goals**:
  - Become a lead UX designer or UX manager.
  - Specialize in an area of UX, such as accessibility, information architecture, or UX research.
  - Contribute to high-impact projects at a major tech company or agency.
  - Transition into UX consulting or freelance work.
  - Build a personal brand in UX, potentially through speaking engagements, publications, or a social media presence.
- **Short-Term Goals**:
  - Complete relevant UX courses or certifications.
  - Build a strong, diverse portfolio that showcases your design and problem-solving skills.
  - Gain experience with industry-standard tools like Figma, Sketch, and Adobe XD.
  - Network with other UX professionals and join design communities.
  - Land an entry-level UX role or internship to gain hands-on experience.

3. Setting SMART Objectives for Your UX Career

Once you've identified your goals, you need actionable objectives that will bring you closer to those goals. The SMART framework is a widely used method for setting clear, achievable objectives. SMART objectives are:

- **Specific**: Clearly defined and focused.
- **Measurable**: Quantifiable, so you can track progress.
- **Achievable**: Realistic and within your capability.
- **Relevant**: Aligned with your long-term career goals.
- **Time-Bound**: Set with a clear timeframe for completion.

Examples of SMART Objectives for UX Designers:

- **Build a Portfolio**: "Within six months, complete and showcase three UX case studies in my portfolio that demonstrate my ability to solve design challenges, conduct user research, and create effective wireframes and prototypes."
- **Develop Research Skills**: "Attend two workshops on user research methodologies

within the next three months and apply those techniques in at least one project."
- **Networking**: "Join two UX design communities within the next month and aim to connect with at least five professionals in the field each month."
- **Master UX Tools**: "Within the next four months, become proficient in Figma by completing a course and applying it to three design projects."

Setting SMART objectives allows you to take manageable steps toward your goals, making the journey feel structured and achievable.

4. Mapping Out the Steps for a UX Career Roadmap

After defining your goals and objectives, create a roadmap that includes practical steps to reach them. Consider dividing your roadmap into different stages, with each stage building on the previous one. Here's an example of what a roadmap might look like for a beginner in UX design:

- **Stage 1: Building Foundational Knowledge**
    - Take introductory courses in UX principles, design thinking, and user research.

- Familiarize yourself with design software, such as Figma, Sketch, or Adobe XD.
- Complete small projects (even if they're hypothetical) to understand basic UX workflows.
- **Stage 2: Developing Practical Skills**
  - Undertake a capstone project or a design challenge to apply your knowledge.
  - Practice creating wireframes, prototypes, and conducting user research.
  - Start building a portfolio, documenting your process, insights, and results.
- **Stage 3: Gaining Real-World Experience**
  - Apply for internships, entry-level roles, or freelance opportunities to gain hands-on experience.
  - Attend UX conferences, webinars, and workshops to learn from industry experts.
  - Seek feedback on your work from mentors or online design communities.
- **Stage 4: Specializing and Growing**
  - Identify a UX specialty you're interested in, such as UX research or interaction design.
  - Pursue additional certifications or courses in your chosen specialty.
  - Build a network of peers, mentors, and potential collaborators who can provide guidance and opportunities.

- **Stage 5: Advancing Your Career**
  - Aim for mid-level UX roles or apply for positions that offer more responsibility.
  - Continue expanding your portfolio with high-quality case studies and complex projects.
  - Stay updated on UX trends and continuously refine your skills through ongoing education.

5. Leveraging Resources and Support Systems

The journey to building a successful UX career is more manageable with the right resources and support. Many platforms, mentors, and communities are available to support UX designers at all stages of their careers.

- **Online Courses and Certifications**: Platforms like Coursera, Udemy, and Interaction Design Foundation (IDF) offer affordable courses, while Google and Nielsen Norman Group provide well-recognized certifications.
- **Mentorship Programs**: Platforms like ADPList, RookieUp, and UXPA's mentorship programs offer mentorship connections. A mentor can provide invaluable guidance, feedback, and career advice.

- **UX Communities and Events**: Joining communities like Designer Hangout (Slack), UX Stack Exchange, and LinkedIn groups can help you network, gain insights, and share knowledge.
- **Books and Blogs**: Keep learning with books like *"Don't Make Me Think"* by Steve Krug, *"The Design of Everyday Things"* by Don Norman, and UX blogs like Smashing Magazine and Nielsen Norman Group's blog.

6. Measuring Progress and Adapting Your Roadmap

A career roadmap is a living document. Regularly review and adapt your goals based on your progress, feedback, and the evolving landscape of UX design. Set aside time every few months to evaluate your roadmap. Ask yourself:

- **Have I achieved my short-term goals?** If not, identify areas to focus on or adjust your timeframe if necessary.
- **Are there new skills I need to develop?** Stay informed about emerging UX trends and determine if you need to incorporate them into your learning.
- **Am I enjoying the journey?** Ensure that your goals align with your interests and

strengths, allowing you to pursue a career that is both fulfilling and sustainable.

A well-thought-out career roadmap is a powerful tool in UX design. By setting clear goals, creating actionable objectives, and staying adaptable, you can navigate your journey with confidence. Remember that a career in UX is not a straight line; it's a dynamic and evolving field that rewards continuous learning and adaptability. Embrace your growth, celebrate small victories, and keep moving forward toward a fulfilling UX career.

Chapter 18

Networking and Freelancing in UX: Insights and Strategies

Networking and freelancing are invaluable in a UX designer's career, opening doors to new opportunities, collaborations, and a wealth of knowledge from industry peers. The UX design field is vast and ever-evolving, and cultivating connections can not only lead to job offers and freelance gigs but also provide support as you grow and adapt. This chapter delves into essential strategies for networking effectively in UX, tips for launching a successful freelancing career, and practical advice on building strong, lasting professional relationships.

1. Why Networking Matters in UX Design

Networking plays a crucial role in helping UX designers learn about industry trends, access job opportunities, and receive mentorship. It goes beyond just meeting people; effective networking in UX is about creating genuine relationships, sharing insights, and supporting each other's career journeys. Networking is especially valuable for freelancers, as it can connect them with potential clients, collaborators, and fellow designers.

Key Benefits of Networking for UX Designers:

- **Learning and Growth**: Gain insights into design tools, processes, and best practices from other professionals.
- **Job and Project Opportunities**: Many UX positions and freelance projects are filled through referrals.
- **Mentorship and Guidance**: Experienced designers can offer feedback on your portfolio, share career advice, and help you navigate challenges.
- **Building a Personal Brand**: Engaging with others in the UX community can help establish you as a knowledgeable professional in your field.

2. Networking Strategies for UX Designers

Building a strong network takes time and consistency. Here are a few strategies to help you build connections effectively:

- **Join UX Communities**: Participate in online communities and forums focused on UX design. Platforms like Designer Hangout (Slack), UX Stack Exchange, and LinkedIn groups offer spaces to ask questions, share knowledge, and learn from peers.
- **Attend Conferences and Meetups**: Attending UX conferences, local meetups, or virtual webinars allows you to connect with others in real-time. Some popular events include the Interaction Design Association (IxDA) conference, UXPA events, and Awwwards conferences.
- **Engage on Social Media**: LinkedIn, Twitter, and Instagram are popular platforms for connecting with other UX designers. Share your work, comment on others' posts, and join conversations around UX topics to build your presence.
- **Leverage LinkedIn**: Use LinkedIn not only to post your achievements but to actively engage with content in your field. Reaching out with personalized connection requests, commenting thoughtfully on industry posts, and sharing relevant content can increase your visibility and build a professional network.
- **Find a Mentor or Be a Mentor**: Many successful designers credit their mentors for

helping them achieve career milestones. Platforms like ADPList connect aspiring UX designers with mentors, while offering mentorship yourself is a great way to give back and build connections.
- **Participate in UX Design Challenges**: Design challenges allow you to showcase your skills and receive feedback. Platforms like Dribbble, Behance, and UX Design Weekly often feature challenges, and participating can help you meet others in the community.

3. Freelancing in UX: Getting Started

Freelancing in UX design offers flexibility, variety, and the chance to work with a diverse range of clients. However, it also requires self-discipline, a business mindset, and strategic networking to build a steady stream of work.

Steps to Start Freelancing in UX:

- **Define Your Services**: Be clear about the UX services you offer. Common services include user research, wireframing, prototyping, usability testing, and visual design. Knowing your strengths will help you target clients who need your specific skills.

- **Build a Strong Portfolio**: Your portfolio is crucial in freelancing, as it's often the deciding factor for potential clients. Showcase diverse projects that highlight your ability to solve design problems and create user-centered experiences. Include case studies that explain your design process, from research to testing.
- **Set Your Rates and Scope**: Pricing can be a challenge, especially when you're starting out. Research market rates for your experience level and services, and consider your expenses and project duration. Remember to define your project scope clearly in contracts to avoid scope creep.
- **Find Clients Through Multiple Channels**: Networking plays a big role here, but you can also find clients on freelance marketplaces (e.g., Upwork, Fiverr, Toptal) and by approaching companies directly. Build relationships with potential clients through LinkedIn or at industry events.
- **Develop Business Skills**: Freelancing involves much more than design work; you'll need to handle client communication, manage projects, and understand basic contracts and invoicing. Consider learning about business essentials for freelancers to set yourself up for long-term success.

4. Best Practices for Freelancing in UX

Freelancing can be unpredictable, but following these best practices can help create a stable and successful freelance career:

- **Communicate Clearly with Clients**: Strong communication is key to freelance success. Set clear expectations from the beginning, establish regular check-ins, and keep your clients updated on project progress.
- **Create Detailed Contracts**: A clear, written contract protects both you and the client by outlining the scope of work, payment terms, timeline, and any necessary deliverables. This helps prevent misunderstandings and ensures you are fairly compensated.
- **Respect Your Time and Set Boundaries**: Freelancers often face the challenge of clients expecting round-the-clock availability. Set boundaries by defining your work hours, response times, and preferred methods of communication in your contract.
- **Manage Finances Wisely**: Freelance income can be irregular, so it's essential to budget carefully and set aside money for taxes. Consider using invoicing tools like FreshBooks or QuickBooks to streamline your finances and keep track of payments.

- **Build a Client Base Through Referrals**: Freelance clients often come through referrals. Do exceptional work, ask for testimonials, and follow up with past clients periodically. Satisfied clients are more likely to refer you to others or rehire you for future projects.
- **Continue Learning and Improving**: Freelancers who consistently learn and improve their skills are better positioned to attract high-quality clients. Take time to upskill, whether through courses, UX bootcamps, or studying industry trends.

5. Staying Competitive as a Freelancer and Networking Strategically

Freelancers face competition, but standing out is possible with a strategic approach to networking and personal branding.

- **Share Your Expertise**: Establish yourself as a knowledgeable UX professional by sharing insights on social media, writing blog posts, or giving talks at industry events. This visibility can help attract clients and connect you with peers who share your interests.
- **Network with Other Freelancers**: Networking isn't limited to finding clients; connecting with other freelancers can lead to

collaboration opportunities, referrals, and support. You might find freelance communities on platforms like Freelancers Union, or through local design groups.
- **Request and Display Client Feedback**: Positive client testimonials on your portfolio or LinkedIn profile can be powerful. These endorsements give potential clients confidence in your work quality and professionalism.
- **Diversify Your Client Base**: Relying on one or two clients can be risky. Aim to work with clients from different industries and of varying sizes to create a stable stream of work.

6. Navigating the Challenges of Freelancing and Networking

While freelancing in UX can be rewarding, it has its challenges. Freelancers often face feast-or-famine work cycles, client disagreements, and the need for self-discipline. To navigate these challenges, you may need to seek ongoing mentorship, continuously improve your skills, and be adaptable to the evolving needs of clients and the UX industry.

Common Challenges and How to Overcome Them:

- **Inconsistent Income**: To address this, build an emergency fund, diversify your income with side projects, and consider offering retainer services for ongoing work.
- **Finding Clients**: Use a mix of networking, online platforms, and referrals to build a steady client pipeline.
- **Handling Difficult Clients**: Clear communication and a detailed contract can prevent many conflicts. If a client becomes difficult, handle the situation professionally and, if necessary, part ways respectfully.

Networking and freelancing are complementary aspects of a UX career that can greatly enhance your experience and success in the field. Effective networking connects you with peers, mentors, and clients, while freelancing allows you to shape your career with flexibility and creativity. By following these strategies, building genuine relationships, and staying proactive in your field, you can create a successful, fulfilling UX career that's grounded in both stability and growth.

Chapter 19

The Future of UX Design: Trends and Technologies to Watch

The world of UX design is rapidly evolving, shaped by new technologies, changing user expectations, and a deepening focus on user-centered design. As designers strive to create more engaging, efficient, and meaningful experiences, staying informed about emerging trends and technologies is essential. This chapter explores key trends that are expected to shape the future of UX design, from artificial intelligence and virtual reality to accessibility, inclusivity, and beyond.

1. The Rise of AI and Machine Learning in UX

Artificial Intelligence (AI) and machine learning are transforming the ways designers approach user experience. These technologies enable more personalized and predictive interactions, allowing UX designers to create adaptive interfaces that respond to individual user preferences and behaviors.

AI Applications in UX Design:

- **Personalization**: AI can deliver tailored content, recommendations, and product suggestions by analyzing user data. This creates a more relevant and engaging experience for each individual.
- **Conversational Interfaces**: Chatbots and virtual assistants powered by AI are becoming essential to UX, providing users with instant support and interaction. As these technologies improve, they will provide increasingly human-like and responsive experiences.
- **Predictive Design**: Machine learning models can anticipate user needs and streamline interfaces, making digital interactions smoother and more intuitive. For instance, a predictive system might prioritize content or features based on past behavior.

For designers, understanding AI and its impact on user behavior will be essential for creating experiences that are both efficient and empathetic.

2. Voice-User Interfaces (VUIs) and Conversational UX

Voice interfaces are becoming a staple in modern UX design as more users engage with voice-activated devices like Amazon Alexa, Google Assistant, and Apple's Siri. These interfaces offer hands-free convenience and accessibility for a broad range of users.

Implications of VUIs in UX Design:

- **Natural Language Processing (NLP)**: As NLP technology advances, voice interfaces can understand and respond more accurately to user queries, which enhances user satisfaction.
- **Context-Aware Design**: VUIs need to respond based on context. Designers must consider how to build systems that understand the user's environment, preferences, and intent.
- **Inclusive Design**: Voice interfaces are especially beneficial for users with visual impairments or mobility limitations. Prioritizing voice as an option can make digital experiences more accessible and inclusive.

3. Virtual Reality (VR) and Augmented Reality (AR) in UX

VR and AR technologies are redefining digital interaction, opening new possibilities for immersive experiences across industries like retail, education, and entertainment.

Key AR/VR Trends for UX Designers:

- **Enhanced User Engagement**: AR and VR can create deeply engaging experiences, such as virtual shopping environments or immersive training simulations. In these spaces, UX designers play a critical role in making interactions intuitive and enjoyable.
- **Spatial UX Design**: Designing for VR and AR requires a spatial understanding, as users interact with virtual elements within a 3D space. This shift means UX designers must learn new skills in spatial arrangement and user movement patterns.
- **Practical Applications**: As AR technology is integrated into mobile devices, users can now experience augmented reality without special hardware. For example, interior design apps use AR to help users visualize furniture placement, and educational apps offer interactive, 3D experiences.

With VR and AR set to become more accessible, designers will need to balance novelty with usability to make these experiences practical and beneficial for users.

4. The Internet of Things (IoT) and UX

The Internet of Things connects various devices, enabling them to share data and work together seamlessly. UX design for IoT presents unique challenges, as experiences extend beyond screens and into the real world.

IoT Considerations for UX Designers:

- **Cross-Device Interactions**: IoT relies on interactions across multiple devices, from smartphones and tablets to smart home systems and wearables. Designers must consider how users will move between these devices and ensure a seamless, cohesive experience.
- **Data Security and Privacy**: With IoT collecting vast amounts of personal data, UX designers must prioritize transparency and privacy settings to build user trust.
- **Proactive User Assistance**: IoT devices can predict user needs and offer proactive assistance, such as adjusting home lighting based on time of day. These anticipatory designs

require a delicate balance to avoid overstepping user boundaries.

As IoT devices become more prevalent, UX designers will need to understand the broader networked ecosystem to create cohesive and secure experiences.

5. Accessibility and Inclusivity as Core UX Principles

As awareness of diversity and inclusion grows, designing for accessibility and inclusivity is no longer optional—it's a requirement. Accessibility will increasingly focus not only on physical and cognitive needs but also on ensuring that everyone, regardless of their background, can enjoy equitable access to technology.

Future Accessibility Trends:

- **Advanced Accessibility Features**: Screen readers, voice controls, and adaptable color schemes will become more sophisticated, helping users of all abilities navigate digital spaces.
- **Designing for Neurodiversity**: Recognizing neurodiversity in UX design, such as designing for users with autism or ADHD, is an emerging focus. This includes creating calm,

non-distracting interfaces and allowing personalization.
- **Global Inclusivity**: With the global reach of digital products, inclusivity also involves designing for different cultural contexts and languages. This approach goes beyond translation; it requires sensitivity to local symbols, colors, and design preferences.

By placing accessibility and inclusivity at the forefront, designers can create products that genuinely serve and respect all users.

6. The Growth of Ethical UX and Privacy-Centered Design

As digital products become more integral to daily life, designers have a responsibility to prioritize ethical considerations and user privacy. UX is shifting to address concerns around data security, user manipulation, and transparent design.

Ethical Design Trends:

- **Data Privacy as a UX Feature**: Rather than burying privacy settings, forward-thinking UX designs prioritize transparency, allowing users to easily control and understand data usage.
- **Dark Pattern Avoidance**: Ethical UX emphasizes avoiding manipulative design

tactics, such as confusing opt-outs or guilt-inducing popups. Users increasingly expect brands to respect their choices and autonomy.
- **Sustainable Design**: With rising environmental awareness, designers are considering sustainability in UX. This might involve reducing data-heavy features that consume energy, minimizing update demands, and encouraging responsible digital consumption.

Ethical UX is about creating products that align with user values, respect their privacy, and offer transparent, honest interactions.

7. Minimalism and Focused Functionality

In an age of information overload, users appreciate simple, streamlined designs that help them focus on essential tasks. Minimalism isn't just a visual trend; it's a response to users' desire for straightforward, distraction-free experiences.

Minimalism Trends in UX Design:

- **Progressive Disclosure**: Designers can prevent overwhelming users by showing information only as it's needed, guiding them step-by-step through complex tasks.

- **Decluttering Interfaces**: Minimalist design focuses on only the most crucial elements, using space wisely to create visually calm, user-friendly layouts.
- **Designing for Focus**: With the rise of productivity tools, UX designers are creating interfaces that encourage focus by reducing notifications, animations, and other potential distractions.

Minimalist, functional design can improve usability and create a sense of calm, making digital interactions more enjoyable and efficient.

8. Embracing Continuous Learning and Adaptability

As new tools, platforms, and methods continue to emerge, UX designers must commit to lifelong learning. Skills such as understanding data analytics, mastering new prototyping tools, and staying informed about changing user expectations will ensure that UX designers remain adaptable in this dynamic field.

The future of UX is exciting and filled with opportunities to create impactful, innovative designs that enhance users' lives. As technology continues to evolve, the role of a UX designer will expand to include empathy-driven, adaptable, and responsible practices. By staying informed about emerging trends and refining their skills, designers can prepare for a future where UX is more powerful, inclusive, and essential than ever.

Appendices

A. Glossary of UX and UI Terms

Understanding key terms is essential for navigating the UX and UI field. Here are some foundational definitions:

- **User Experience (UX)**: The overall experience a user has when interacting with a product, focusing on ease of use, accessibility, and pleasure.
- **User Interface (UI)**: The visual aspects of a product that allow users to interact with it, such as buttons, icons, and layout.
- **Wireframe**: A simple, low-fidelity outline or blueprint of a digital product, showing the basic structure and layout without visual details.
- **Prototype**: An early, interactive version of a design used for testing and feedback before final development.
- **Usability**: The degree to which a product is easy to use and effective in helping users achieve their goals.
- **Persona**: A fictional character created to represent a specific user type, helping designers empathize with their needs and behaviors.
- **Accessibility**: Designing products so that all users, including those with disabilities, can use them effectively.

- **Information Architecture (IA)**: The organization and structure of content within a product to ensure it's logically presented and easy to navigate.
- **User Journey**: A sequence of steps a user takes to complete a task within a product, mapped out to identify pain points and optimize the experience.
- **Design Thinking**: A user-centered approach to problem-solving in UX design, emphasizing empathy, ideation, prototyping, and testing.

B. Recommended Reading and Learning Resources

To dive deeper into UX design, consider the following books and resources:

- **Books**:
  - *"Don't Make Me Think" by Steve Krug*: A classic on usability and user-centered design principles.
  - *"The Design of Everyday Things" by Don Norman*: Explores the psychological aspects of design and usability.

- *"Lean UX" by Jeff Gothelf and Josh Seiden*: Discusses collaborative UX approaches in agile teams.
- *"100 Things Every Designer Needs to Know About People" by Susan Weinschenk*: Offers insights on how people think, feel, and behave when using products.
- **Websites**:
  - *Nielsen Norman Group* (www.nngroup.com): Research, articles, and reports on UX design best practices.
  - *A List Apart* (alistapart.com): Articles on design, development, and UX insights.
  - *Interaction Design Foundation* (interaction-design.org): Courses, articles, and resources covering various UX topics.
- **Online Courses**:
  - *Coursera and edX*: Offer UX design courses from universities such as Stanford and the University of Michigan.
  - *LinkedIn Learning*: Short, practical courses on UX/UI tools and principles.
  - *Google UX Design Certificate*: A beginner-friendly course designed to build foundational UX skills.

C. Example UX Design Project Framework

When approaching a UX project, a structured framework can help guide your process. Here's an example framework:

1. **Define the Problem**: Identify the problem the design needs to solve.
2. **Conduct User Research**: Use methods like interviews, surveys, and user testing to understand user needs.
3. **Create User Personas**: Develop personas to represent different user types and inform design decisions.
4. **Develop User Journeys**: Map out the user's interaction flow and identify pain points.
5. **Wireframing and Prototyping**: Design low-fidelity wireframes, then move to interactive prototypes.
6. **Usability Testing**: Conduct tests with real users, gather feedback, and refine the design.
7. **Iterate and Finalize**: Make improvements based on feedback and finalize the design for development.

D. Portfolio Templates and Example Layouts

Your portfolio is critical for showcasing your skills and approach. Here are tips and templates:

- **Essential Sections**:
  - **About Me**: Describe your background, skills, and approach to UX design.
  - **Case Studies**: Include detailed project breakdowns with visuals, showcasing the problem, process, and solutions.
  - **Skills and Tools**: List software skills, research methods, and technical competencies.
  - **Contact Information**: Make it easy for potential employers or clients to reach you.
- **Portfolio Templates**:
  - **Adobe Portfolio**: Customizable templates with integration for Adobe XD and Photoshop projects.
  - **Behance**: A widely used platform for showcasing design projects.
  - **Webflow and Wix**: Offers easy-to-use, customizable templates tailored for designers.

When building layouts, prioritize simplicity, readability, and strong visuals to make your work stand out.

E. Suggested Design Exercises and Mini-Projects

Practicing with small projects and exercises can sharpen your UX skills:

1. **Redesign a Common Interface**: Pick an app you use daily and create a new design that addresses any usability issues you encounter.
2. **Develop User Personas**: Identify a target user type and create a persona, considering their demographics, motivations, and challenges.
3. **Conduct a Usability Test**: Take a simple website or app and run a usability test with friends or family. Note feedback and identify areas for improvement.
4. **Wireframing Practice**: Choose a website or app you like, and create wireframes for its main pages to understand layout and structure.
5. **User Journey Mapping**: Map the steps a user takes to complete a goal in an app, highlighting any pain points or friction areas.

These exercises will help build both your technical and empathy skills as a designer.

F. Common UX Design Mistakes to Avoid

Being aware of common pitfalls can help you create better, more user-centered designs:

- **Ignoring User Research**: Skipping research leads to designs based on assumptions, which may not meet user needs.
- **Overloading with Features**: Avoid adding too many features at once; prioritize simplicity and essential functionalities.
- **Inconsistent UI Elements**: Keep colors, fonts, and buttons consistent to maintain user familiarity and prevent confusion.
- **Neglecting Accessibility**: Design for users with diverse abilities by following accessibility best practices.
- **Poor Navigation Design**: Ensure that navigation is intuitive, consistent, and predictable to avoid user frustration.

Recognizing these mistakes early can help you create designs that are both functional and delightful.

G. UX Design Communities and Networking Resources

Building connections with other UX designers can provide support, inspiration, and career opportunities. Here are some valuable communities:

- **Online Forums**:
  - **Designer Hangout**: A Slack community for UX designers to discuss design, career advice, and industry trends.
  - **UX Design Subreddit (r/userexperience)**: A Reddit community for questions, case studies, and general UX discussions.
- **Professional Groups**:
  - **AIGA (American Institute of Graphic Arts)**: Hosts UX design events, workshops, and networking opportunities.

- **UXPA (User Experience Professionals Association)**: Offers resources, local meetups, and an annual UX conference.
- **Social Media and Networking**:
  - **LinkedIn**: Join UX design groups and follow industry leaders to stay updated.
  - **Twitter**: Follow hashtags like #uxdesign, #userexperience, and #designthinking to discover tips, discussions, and the latest trends.

Joining these communities provides access to mentorship, knowledge-sharing, and feedback that can be instrumental in advancing your UX career.

www.ingramcontent.com/pod-product-compliance
Lightning Source LLC
Chambersburg PA
CBHW071455220526
45472CB00003B/806